KING OF CLUBS

SEX, DRUGS AND THUGS –
THE ONE NATION STORY

TERRY TURBO

Monday Books

© Terry Turbo 2006

First published in Great Britain in 2006 by Monday Books

The right of Terry Turbo to be identified as the Author
of this work has been asserted by him in accordance with the
Copyrights, Designs and Patents Act 1988

A CIP catalogue record for this title is available
from the British Library

ISBN 0-9552854-3-7
(2007 ISBN: 9780955285431)

Typeset in Times by Avon Dataset Ltd,
Bidford On Avon, Warwickshire

Printed and bound by Creative Print & Design Group,
Harmondsworth, Middlesex

www.mondaybooks.com
info@mondaybooks.com

Terry Turbo worked with Stuart Wheatman on King of Clubs. Stuart lives with his family in the North East.

His other books include *Cage Fighter* and *The Krays – The Geordie Connection*.

He also publishes and can be found at www.tontopress.com

Contents

Dedication

This book is dedicated to my Nan – rest in peace! – and my Mum, Maxine and Alfie, Jade, my brother Philip, all the One Nation security team for looking after me, Wilf Pine – you've been a real father to me, thanks pops – all my real friends (you know who you are) and all the One Nation and Garage Nation ravers who have supported me over the years.

God bless you all.

Terry, November 2006.

Wilf's Foreword

I got together with Terry in about 1995 through a mutual acquaintance. I'd already heard a lot about him; I think you had to be on another planet not to. When I met him, I'd been heavily involved in a lot of things, as well as the music scene. If anyone remembers a little band called Black Sabbath, I used to manage them, and you may already be aware of some of my other activities, too.

In meeting Terry, I met a special guy. It was just like looking at me 30 years ago, but he was a lot cleverer than me because he took a different path with his life. If he'd tried management, the energy he possessed would have been enough to make anyone a star. He may still do that one day, who knows? I've joked with him many a time that he would have made a brilliant criminal and I'm so glad he's never tried to prove me right.

I feel proud to know him and proud to have watched him grow over the years and become the biggest promoter in the country. That didn't happen through chance. He earned the respect of his peers by winning awards for his work and earned respect from the chaps by his conduct and reputation. Terry is more than capable of having a row with anyone and still go back for more. Those are great qualities, and ones you need as a promoter. He carries himself with confidence and the bloke oozes charisma – a perfect gentleman.

If I had another son, I'd wish it to have been Terry. I'm honoured to be the one he turns to for advice, and like a dad, I've been able to help him out from time to time if he's needed it. He's got so much self-belief and is such a strong character that no one could break him as a promoter or as a person. Even when the shit was piled up against him, he came out smelling of roses. He's an absolute superstar; and you know what, in my eyes he's been that for years already. No one can stop Terry – only he can. If he feels something is wrong, he'll stop, rethink and change direction or put it to bed.

Terry has always been a tough guy. The difference between him and all the other ones is that he's got a brain, and that's why, I can rest, safe in the knowledge that he'll always be a survivor.

God bless you, Terry.

Your mate,

Wilf Pine, November 2006.

Terry's Foreword

Raving. Out of your head on a massive high. A million megawatts of lasers firing purple, green and red lines of pure light through the dry ice and the smoke and the steam. Women in hotpants and vests bouncing all around you. The beat, the rhythm, pounding through your body, the bass . . . it's so loud, so deep, that it's rumbling in your chest, making your bones vibrate and shake. The MC shouts something and three thousand kids blow whistles, wave glow sticks and grin, big, face-splitting grins. All around you there's a feeling of love, of togetherness, of *this-is-our-time* . . . in your head, in your heart, in your soul.

Raving. Trust me, there's no feeling in the world like it.

And then, one day, you wake up and it's *your* rave. Three thousand punters out of their heads. Dealers walking round with bags of E and whizz. DJs turning up late and trying to smuggle in guns. Birds on their knees, giving the doormen blow jobs so they can get in free.

There's muggers steaming through your venue beating people up and robbing them, and gangsta-wannabes are waving pistols around outside because you won't let them in for nothing.

It's all about to go off, big-time.

And you've got a hundred thousand pounds of your very own, very hard-earned money riding on all of this.

Now you're a promoter.

There ain't many feelings in the world like that, either.

I started out the first way, and I ended up the second. Along the road, I had a lot of laughs, a lot of thrills and a lot of very scary moments. How and why I'm still alive to tell this tale, I don't know. Somebody, somewhere, must be looking out for me.

This is my story: the story of One Nation, the biggest and best club promoters in the whole wide world . . . about how we gave 10 million and more ravers a great time, every time.

Well, I would say that, wouldn't I?

GETTING AN EDUCATION

OK, let's get the obvious out the way first; why Terry Turbo? There are all sorts of rumours about how I came by the name . . . because I've knocked a few people out very quickly . . . because I'm always on the move, always busy . . . because I've driven a few turbo-charged cars.

Sadly, it's not quite that glamorous.

It came from the days of break dancing. To be precise, *Break Dance: The Movie*, an old skool classic (featuring Jean-Claude Van Damme as an extra in a rather fetching black leotard during the beach dance-off scene). One of the main characters, played by Michael 'Boogaloo Shrimp' Chambers, was called Turbo. I was a break dancer, so everyone started calling me Turbo Terry. They were taking the piss, of course, and I fucking hated it. But because it got a reaction from me, it stuck; after a while, I realised I was never going to get shake it off, so I accepted it. In the end, Turbo became a brand name and even grew on me over the years. Kind of.

That's where my story begins – with the baptism of Turbo Terry. Or Terry Turbo, as I eventually became.

I was in my early teens when the film came out, and me and my mates used to break dance outside Bracknell shopping centre, having dance-offs with other crews in the area. We even went to classes run by the GMC break dancers in a squash court in the Arena sports centre in Camberley, to hone our truly awful skills.

I lived on a council estate in Camberley, the Old Dean. It was

1

rough then and it's rougher now; back then, we broke a few windows and nicked bits and pieces from the sweet shop. Now, kids are being stabbed to death over nothing and drugs and gang violence are the norm.

Ever since the early days, it's been me, my mum and my Nan, when she was alive. My mum and dad split up when I was young. He was an alcoholic and a womaniser – he had a great job and a great wife but he pissed it all away, going from being a regional manager at one of the biggest supermarket chains in the country to being a taxi driver. I'm not knocking taxi drivers, I'm just saying he could have had everything he wanted in life and he threw it all away for alcohol. I saw the damage that addiction can cause from an early age and I didn't like what I saw. I could understand doing something that was good for you and made you stronger, but doing something that tears your family apart and makes you ill or kills you . . . that I couldn't get my head round. I wasted a lot of time trying to keep in touch with him but nothing ever came back: no 18th birthday card, nothing for my 21st. So I fucked him off in the end, and I don't speak to him now. When they separated, me and mum moved, and I had to go to a new school. They weren't great days, early on. You know what bullies are like: if you're new, or you're not wearing the right trainers, or you wear glasses, they'll zone in on your weakness. I wasn't a confident kid. I was skinny and little for my age and I got bullied a fair bit. I didn't have that father figure to inspire me, tell me how it was, show me how to put my hands up and protect myself. I had my mum and my Nan round me, and they were into nice stuff like going swimming, not scrapping and violence. I spent a good few years being frightened of the bullies, frightened of getting hurt, frightened of fighting. I remember one kid in particular. Mark Tyson was his name, and he was a right prick. His favourite thing was to walk up to you and punch you in the mouth. No reason, no warning, just . . . bang! Tyson did that to me a couple of times and eventually, what with everything else going on, I realised I needed to learn how to look after myself. I went down to the Camberley Amateur Boxing Club and said I wanted to join. They obviously had a lot of this; the guy said, 'Yeah, you and everyone else . . . OK, you can come here and watch. If you still here after three weeks, and you're still interested, you can have a go.'

So I went and watched. I remember thinking, *I'm not sure if I actually fancy this* but I was still going round three weeks later so they let me join. I was 14. Once I worked out that getting hit in the face does hurt but it's not the end of the world, I loved it. Six months or so into the boxing, I was stronger, fitter and much more confident.

I was in assembly one morning and this kid called Lawrence Larby started having a go at me. Mark Tyson was a mate of his and he was sitting in front; he just turned round and punched me in the face, in assembly, in front of everyone.

I said, 'You fucking cunt.'

He started going, 'Yeah, me and you outside, later.'

I said, 'No, me and you now.'

And I went for him, and started smashing the fuck out of him. I really went to town on him, there was blood and teeth everywhere, and he had nothing to come back with. The teachers let me get on with it – they all knew he was a bully – and I never had any more trouble with him or anyone else afterwards. Ironically, when I started going out raving four or five years later, I bumped into him a few times and he was all, 'Alright Tel, how's it going?', like he was my best mate. Like I said: a right prick.

I learned a couple of important lessons from Mark Tyson.

Firstly, I learned that most people, even those who look and act hard, can't actually fight. They've got no discipline, they just flail around and they don't know how to make you miss. Once you've stood toe-to-toe with another boxer in a ring a few times, you're way ahead of the average Joe; the chances are that if you give them a good shot in the face you'll knock them out.

Secondly, I learned that bullies are full of shit. Once they've been given a good hiding, they don't want to know.

Boxing was really important to me, a great way for me to improve my endurance and test my character. From about 15, I started fighting for Camberley. I was so nervous ahead of my first fight that I spent the day puking up, right up to the first bell. I was probably dehydrated, and I lost on points. After that, I knew I'd lose them all if I didn't focus on winning – mind over matter, and all that – so I changed my mental approach and that helped a lot. I also changed clubs, moving to Pinewood Star, which was quite a famous set-up. It was run by a guy called Les Stevens, who'd boxed John Conteh before he won the title. A lot of good fighters came from the club – Georgie and Tony Collins and Les's son, Blue Stevens, who won the heavyweight ABA title. My fourth fight was the Surrey Schoolboys Final. I was up against a kid who was ranked number four in the country. He'd had nearly 60 fights compared to my four and he beat me on points, but I'm proud to say he didn't put me down and I went at him for the whole fight. The guy's name was Richard Williams – since then, he's won Commonwealth and IBO titles so I think I can be proud of my showing. My record stood at eight fights, five wins and three losses when I packed it in.

I was a keen cross-country runner, too, and I got into hill-running for a while. I loved being fit and it gave me something to do with my time. It was that, or drift towards crime like a lot of the other kids on my estate. The Old Dean was the pits back then and, like I say, it's even worse today. *The Sun* carried a big story on it a while back under the headline *Hell Estate Is Starved Of Cops*. It said families were being plagued by vandals, racists, drug-users and burglars. It's a right fucking dangerous place. At school one morning the PE teacher approached me, absolutely buzzing, saying he'd seen me running the night before and was amazed; he asked me to join the cross-country team and my first appearance was in the Surrey Schools County Cross Country Championships. Our school got first, second, fourth and fifth places – I came fifth, not bad for my first ever race. I wasn't Kip Keno but I was given a certificate, which I've still got.

4

Chuffed to bits, I was. I needed things like that to boost my self-esteem.

Despite all that, I still got into trouble from time to time, like most other lads. I got nicked when I was 14. I was hanging round at the park, watching a group of kids vandalising the community centre. Who needs Playstations when you can watch live vandalism? Before long the police turned up, chased everyone and I got caught and they took me down the clink and called my mum down to see me given a warning – not that I'd actually done anything. Mostly it was just having a laugh. My mum was seeing this builder called Jack – he called himself *Jack the Trowel, The Camberley Cowboy*, with the name down the side of his van and a Stetson on his head – and I used to wind him up all the time. I'd make prank phone calls to him, leave my Nan's potty on the roof of his van and shoot him with my air rifle when he got home drunk.

I left school without any qualifications and no real direction. I wanted to go to Guilford College to do a bricklaying course because I'd done a bit of labouring here and there and I thought being a brickie would be a decent trade to get into. But my mum couldn't afford it, so I went off into the big wide world.

My first – very glamorous – job was at McDonald's in Camberley. We had some right proper laughs there, me and my mate Richard. It was like the Wild West, with gangs of teenage yobs and local pissheads fighting over the burgers; we were forever chucking people out, or throwing their shakes over them or hosing them down with the fire extinguishers. One time, a gang came in and started messing me around, taking the piss. I got one of the lads in the toilets and told him I'd smash him up unless they stopped giving me grief. He was scared on his own but once he was back with all his mates, his balls grew back and it was business as usual . . . 'Get me a burger Turbo Terry, get me a straw Turbo Terry.'

They knew that if I sorted anyone properly I'd get the sack. So I phoned my mate's gang instead; they came in and kicked the

5

shit out of them for me. The cops came down but they couldn't prove I was involved and the lads who were giving me grief in the first place were in no McFlurry to come back for more. Home win to Turbo Terry. *And* I laughed my bollocks off.

I was at Maccy-ds for two years, and ended up as the lobby host, the manager of the dining area. (Didn't I do well . . . this goes out to all the teachers that said I'd never make it!)

But my fast food career came to an end when two well-to-do couples, dressed in dinner jackets and elegant ball gowns, walked in late one night and ordered burgers and fries amid the usual yobbery and chaos. Were they lost? Or having a laugh? Who knows? Anyway, they complained about some geezer's swearing. What they wanted me to do about it, I don't know. One of the lad's mates swaggered over to their table, pulled out his knob and dipped it in their ketchup. Then he wrote his name on the table with it.

The four posh punters upped and walked out, with a lot of jeering and abuse helping them on their way. I pissed myself laughing. Well, it was funny. Pity my boss didn't see it that way. The next day he called me into his office and asked me why I hadn't stopped the yob with the knob. I gave an honest answer. 'I'd never seen anyone act like that before in my life. I was embarrassed and didn't know what to do. All I could do was laugh.'

He demoted me on the spot and my reaction was another honest one – I told him he could stick his job up his Mc-fucking-Arse, and I left with my head held high. I remained good mates with Richard and he's still a partner in one of my other ventures to this day.

I needed to find a job so I thought, *Why not join the Royal Marines*? With all the training I was doing, I knew I was already fit as fuck and ready for a challenge.

I went for the three-day induction, passed all the tests and was sure I was sailing through it, pardon the pun. On the last day, they put me on this thing called the Tarzan Course. It sounds a bit of a giggle, and it probably is if you don't have vertigo. I would rather squeeze my own balls in a vice than climb any higher than three steps and this was the sort of course where you had to throw yourself off platforms and grab onto ropes, all 30 foot up in the air. I quit, something I hate doing. But the fear of heights was too strong and it wasn't to be.

After another rethink, I tried the Navy. It was an absolute fucking disaster. I was under the impression it would be physical exercise 24/7, not seven minutes out of twenty-four hours. How wrong can you be? It was like school, only with classes in ironing clothes, polishing shoes, cleaning everything with a surface, cleaning the surface of every surface, polishing more stuff and a bit more ironing. I woke up a few mornings wondering if I'd actually signed up for the wrong course. Don't get me wrong, the Navy is great if that's the kind of person you are, any service is. I just couldn't see the point. You lift weights to build muscles, you go running to get fit, you work late to get the job done . . . and you iron clothes, shine shoes and polish buttons in order to . . . er . . . represent your country in battle? Ah, it all makes sense now.

I needed to get out but they wouldn't let me go till I'd finished basic training. Six weeks. No way. I started being as awkward as I could – I refused to do any washing or ironing, I didn't clean my shoes or make my bed, I just messed around and gave the instructors a lot of lip. They weren't easy people to convince. They had me cleaning toilets with toothbrushes, watering fields with tiny watering cans and really wishing I was somewhere else.

The Chief PO was a right charmer. 'Me and you are going to go for a walk one night and you're not going to come back,' he said.

Death threats on a training course? And they say bullying doesn't go on in these places. I told him to let me know when he thought he was ready. I'd rather have had a tear-up with him and see what happened than take any more of their shit. *Anything* than clean another bog with a toothbrush.

In the end, I was discharged for not taking any of it seriously. Who was more relieved, me or them, I don't know. One thing I do know is that I learnt another lesson from it.

I learnt never to go into anything again all wide-eyed and innocent, not knowing the full implications. And I learnt something about myself too: that I wasn't the type just to sit back and take orders like some zombie.

I was glad to get home, back to my mum and my Nan, to my own bed and my mum's cooking. We'd always been close and being away from them made me appreciate what I had going for me even more. You hear people talking about how an event helps them 'find themselves' – that was probably mine.

Where I found myself was Allders, cleaning all the TVs and videos and wrapping them up before they went out to customers. (My CV is starting to sound terrible, I know, *and* I've missed some stuff out.) There I was in my Farah slacks, shirt and polyester tie, earning 60 English pounds a week. Not exactly rolling in money; it paid me enough to get by and meant I was earning and not sponging. This was where I started to use my head, where my entrepreneurial skills were beginning to develop.

I'd always had an interest in TVs and cameras and all the other gadgets on the market so it was great to be surrounded by them all day. I did my homework, read up on them and learnt how they all worked. In the end, I probably knew more about them than the sales people did. Armed with my newly-acquired knowledge, I started trying my hand at selling when the sales team were busy. Because I knew my stuff, I could answer the customers' questions and, after a month or so, the manager put me on commission because of how impressed he was with me. There were a few part-time salespeople there who weren't on commission so we got a little scam going: when they rang a sale through, they'd do it on my number. I got the commission, and bought them the odd cup of tea and sticky bun with my riches to make it worth their while.

Pretty soon, and even without these snidey extra sales, I was outselling everyone in there.

I didn't discriminate, or second-guess, or only go for concrete-looking sales . . . I just got stuck in to everyone.

I was learning how to be a people-person, watching their behaviour and learning how to communicate like a pro. Fuck school and qualifications – this was real education.

After I while, I got out of Allders and landed a job as a sales rep for a scaffolding firm in Bracknell. I'd just passed my driving test and my new job came with a decent salary, and a company car with my petrol paid for. This was a big deal: the fact that someone thought I was *worth* giving a car meant they thought I was good at something. You can't beat that feeling; it gave me a huge boost. I went up the repping ladder to a place in Slough – bigger car, more money, mobile phone the size of a brick, £5 a minute for your calls – and I was doing well, living the 80s Yuppie dream. I was probably in danger of drinking in wine bars surrounded by mates called Sebastian and Miranda, wearing a light grey baggy suit, stripy shirt and braces if I wasn't careful. As if. I did spend every penny I earned on clothes and going out drinking and clubbing, though. The day after tomorrow seemed like a million miles away.

The deal with Jack the Trowel was, he'd pay the mortgage and she'd pay the bills. Only the tosser didn't pay the mortgage. Eventually, my mum binned him and we tried to make a go of it on our own. She wanted me to take on the mortgage but I couldn't afford it. Considering any commitment at that time was impossible. I was just starting to come out my shell and discovering life with no ties was the only thing I wanted to devote my time to. I had mates to go out drinking with and girls to chase. In your late teens, the last thing you want is a mortgage hanging round your neck. So the house got repossessed and we ended up being rehoused with my Nan in a council house. It was tough to refuse my mum, and tough when we had to move. But that cloud ended up having a major silver lining.

I was made redundant. It was an instant, shit-hitting-the-fan process which left me out on my arse with nothing.

Redundant – what a horrible word.

And before I was 20 years old. Like I say, there was a small silver lining: if we'd bought the house, we'd have been absolutely stuffed and we'd have lost it anyway.

I was never destined to sit around on my arse but people weren't hiring and the dole queues were growing. I went for dozens of job interviews but I got knocked back from every decent one. My lack of school qualifications didn't help. Their argument was always, *If you can do anything when you put your mind to it, why didn't you put your mind to passing exams*? The age-old exam debate. Works for some people, not for others. I didn't need a piece of paper saying I'd passed a Maths exam to know how many beans made three. Fuck it.

I drifted through a series of things: I was a refuse collection technician (bin man), a produce storage executive (shelf stacker) and a cleaner (sick of my life). I tried my hand at a few ventures of my own. There was the Turbo Hairdressers, which went tits up. My mate and me set up an escort agency which was a total disaster. All he was interested in was shagging the women, and if you're banging them they aren't getting banged by a punter and you're not getting paid. I drafted my mum in to work on the phone – the idea was there, but it was a shambles and we made about £80.

I was temporarily in the gutter, and I knew it, but I was always looking up at the stars. Most people would have called me a daydreamer, but I just knew something was going to come along.

TURBO PROMOTIONS

I'd started going out clubbing when I was about 15. I say 'clubbing': I'm talking your typical high street dive. Ragamuffin's was opposite the McDonald's in Camberley – a real fucking cattle market which had seen better days, wall-to-wall with the Sharons and Traceys of the area, or Shaz and Trace once you got a cider 'n' black in them and were on a promise. We had our pick of every clapped-out old boiler in there, not to mention the smart ones who stumbled in by accident. God help them when we got started. There was another place called Straws and a few others where the doormen had Old Dean Radars and wouldn't let the likes of us lot in. How unfair can you get? Not letting 15-year-olds into a club?

Traditionally, we'd sink a few Special Brews on the way into town, and by the time we got there we were unstoppable and we loved it. I used to spend around a tenner on a night, then most of the next day trying to piece the night together and remember who got laid and who puked where and when. It was always a classy affair and always a right old laugh.

Around then, I had my first experience of proper dance music. When I'd worked at Allders, I'd met a geezer called Chris who told me I had to go to a rave. The way he pitched it to me, it was a life and death situation. He was always getting pilled up and off his face; his Monday morning come-downs weren't exactly a joy to behold but he was always back on it by midweek, banging on about the latest club he'd been to. Who was I to argue?

If going to Sharon and Tracey dives was discovering a new social life, then going raving was like discovering a new civilisation. With a new language. On a new planet. In a new solar system. And I fucking loved it. Balls to all that Normalsville shit – I packed my case and got myself a one-way ticket to Planet Rave.

I drifted apart from the Old Dean crowd in what seemed like no time at all and got in with a bunch of mates through Chris, going to places like the Caribbean Club in Basingstoke and the Rivermead Centre in Reading.

It was the start of an obsession. I bought and listened to all the tapes, consuming them like a madman, losing myself in them and connecting so much with them that I felt like I was part of it. Bollocks, I *was* part of it. Much like when people say they were touched by God and religion, I found myself converted to dance music. I loved the fact that no-one gave a fuck about who you were or where you were from – it was all about the music. Black, white, male or female, it didn't matter. It brought everyone together.

With a new set of mates and wanting to experience different things, I became one half of a dance duo with my mukka Marvellous Marvin Cain. Marvin was the DJ, I was the MC and together we were . . . wait for it . . . Two Tone. He was black (still is) and I was and am white, hence the name. We were going to be the Stevie Wonder and Paul McCartney of dance music, until we discovered that Tone Deaf would have been more appropriate. We did one gig at Perry's in Wokingham. My mum and one of her friends came to see us rock the house. It was great to get some home support and even better to see my mum in the crowd giving it large but, to be honest, we were shocking and we called it a day – more at that difficult second gig stage than that difficult second album. A short-lived venture, Two Tone will always be the dance act that could have been, should have been and never was. Marv carried on for a long time after – well, he was the one with all the talent – and he is now an established music producer and DJ.

I was loving my raving, enjoying discovering this new scene and new way of being, and my Old Dean mates had become nine to fivers who just wanted to get pissed-up on a weekend and have fights. That sort of rubbish had lost its appeal for me. The fighting, anyway. Although I kept myself physically fit, I never had a problem with pouring gallons of alcohol down my neck; all that *my body is a temple* malarkey never interested me.

I soon realised that there were other vices a raver could get into – all those lads in denim dungarees weren't gurning and dancing funny all night for no reason. Every culture has its seedier side and rave culture was no different then, and was on its way to getting a lot worse. But it was only after clubbing for around four months that I really got anywhere near drugs myself. I'd seen all the signs, I wasn't naïve – I knew they existed and knew that a huge percentage of people my age were on them, so it wasn't like it was a shock to me. In my younger days, I'd been around mates having a bit of puff if we were bunking off school. I even tried it, but it wasn't for me – you either take to it or you don't. I didn't see the point in smoking something that made me feel sick.

E was a different ball game.

Like many, I was a bit wary of Es because I'd read too many nightmare stories in the newspapers. It does put you off, but then your mates are fine and so is everybody else in the club, and you're just too curious. Just snap it in half – see what happens . . . a half isn't pushing the boat out too much, is it? And then you neck the other half and have the best night of your life. Your energy levels are up, the music sounds great, you move in perfect rhythm to the beat, you feel so confident, so unbelievably happy and in love with everyone. Weird. But good-weird.

Even though it was a lot of fun, E was never a major thing for me. Like 99% of people, I did it a bit when I was younger, kept it well under control and stopped as I matured.

The thing is – and you don't read about this is the papers – taking drugs *can* be a good experience. Of course, that's a controversial thing to say, and it can be taken out of context. However, like it or not, ecstasy pills, as far as I know, don't make you unreasonable, violent, determined to have a fight, and prone to glassing someone in the neck. In all my years of being in clubs, that never happened – at least, not when someone was 'on one'. All drugs have different effects: people having a smoke just can't be bothered to have a fight, people on acid have turned into a castle full of flying leprechauns, people on a speed and Es are too busy feeling the rush and dancing and hugging. It's the people who've had too much to drink who always want a good row with someone. Even a happy drunk is more susceptible to an argument than usual. As a punter in a rave, I rarely sensed any threat or bad atmosphere – it was the complete opposite because people all had the same intention to have a good time. You couldn't beat that 'no bullshit' atmosphere.

I'd love to get a grant of a few hundred grand. I'd run the most unethical scientific experiment in history on this pro-position: two thousand people on a good pill, in a rave, are almost certain to have a great time, smile a lot, hug each other, dance their arses off and have a memorable night out that they talk about for ages. Two thousand drunken people in a rave are almost certain to start fights with each other for no reason at random intervals throughout the night and not remember any of it. I'd just need to observe and compare the results, maybe correlate a graph or two and run a Mann-Whitney test on it. I assume. It's something I witnessed every weekend, every night out, and I still see it today.

I don't think the authorities would like the results, though; they make billions out of the duty on booze, after all. Alcohol and ecstasy are both drugs, but society says that one is socially acceptable and the other isn't, even though the acceptable one is the bigger killer and leads to violent crime, road traffic deaths and all manner of embarrassing behaviour that you know you're going to regret in the morning. A sweeping statement, I know, but it's true.

I'm not here to preach. These things go on whether we like them or not; they're a part of life. I'm certainly not pro-drugs – I definitely don't think anyone under the age of 18 should go anywhere anything illegal – or anti-alcohol. I've seen plenty of people enjoy a drink harmlessly and some people on the rave scene ended up fucking their lives up completely because they didn't know when enough was enough.

When you try a drug, it doesn't mean you suddenly turn to crack and start stealing from your granny's purse. Recreational drugs are just that. A substitute for getting off your tits on beer, a booster to help you dance all night, a way of expanding your mind . . . everyone has a different reason. Where it goes wrong is when it becomes about the drugs, rather than about using them as an occasional tool to support what you're really there for, the music and the atmosphere.

Like I say, after a while I knocked it on the head. When I was out clubbing I was transformed anyway. I got a natural buzz, and nothing else came close to it; everyone should experience that rush at least once in their life. Raving became my drug of choice. I needed it all the time, wished my working week away, lived for the weekend, and it was obvious it had the same effect on everyone else in there – it was like you could communicate with people telepathically or with a look that summed the music or the laser display up in a second. Everyone in there shared a spiritual connection that I doubt you get in any other sphere of life. Clubbing and raving was all about sharing the moment and sharing the night. Sometimes I thought about the people on the outside who didn't know what they were missing out on . . . a whole subculture uniting all of those who dared to let themselves go, people they'd only ever read about in the tabloids and think were weird.

I never dreamed I'd be able to make a living out of it.

I knew a guy called Nigel Green who was something to do with the sports centre in Basingstoke, and who put on parties called Energy. At a loose end one day, and between jobs, I phoned him up and asked if I could sell tickets for him. I was hoping to make a few quid and get in free to his events. We became mates and I ended up doing other promotional stuff like handing flyers out. He was funny as fuck – he used to get stressed out and collapse all the time. As soon as a conversation got a bit heated, at the first sign of hassle – bang, he was out of it. God knows what the problem was; you could be in a rave with him or having a conversation and the next thing, he'd be on the floor. It was a real conversation stopper.

I used to go around all the record shops for Nigel and make sure there were flyers and posters in all the right places. A lot of the job was networking – getting to know the blokes who ran the shops, talking to them about music, building my contacts up and showing a friendly face for the company. There were coach trips to his events that I used to organise, too. I had the opportunity to learn the ropes with Nigel as a kind of mentor and friend.

It was Nigel who got me interested in promoting. When I saw him collapsing all the time, I thought, *If he can do it*, anyone *can*. And it related to selling and it was dealing directly with people – two things I thrived on. If you can earn a crust from something you like and are good at, that's great. If you are resourceful, a good talker and can think on your feet, then you can promote.

The job wasn't permanent – it was helping out on a casual basis. Yeah, I'd have liked a full-time thing. But the upside was I wasn't tied to Nigel. I spent a few months learning off him, gradually turning my mind towards going it alone.

On the way out of a rave one night, sweating like a pig, I saw a load of lads outside giving flyers out to all the punters leaving the venue. This was the kind of thing I'd been doing with Nigel and I knew these guys – they were The Flying Squad, based in West London. This was how they made their living, distributing flyers for events, target-marketing people who attended raves. People like me.

I approached them and they took me on, in spring 1992. The work was regular weekends and it paid better than Nigel. I could do my own thing through the week and get a couple of free nights out at the weekend and get paid for working afterwards. Making money clubbing instead of spending it – it's the stuff of genius.

Russell was the governor of the company and Danny was the one who did all the running around, though there were rumours that a couple of really heavy duty guys were connected to them called Noah and Kenny. I noticed how those kind of rumours seemed to come in very useful: no-one fucked them around.

If I was flying Thursday or Friday, I'd drive up on the Thursday morning and pick my boxes up from them ready for the evening. The first thing I noticed about doing flyers is that I suddenly became someone people want to know. I'd somehow developed instant magnetism. This was a good chance to really reinvent myself. Handing free stuff out is an on-the-spot chat-up line and an excuse to approach anyone, armed with 100 flyers in one hand and a bag full of ulterior motives in the other. It was all about being spontaneous and improvising around the first thing that popped into my head. Being on board with The Flying Squad was cool because they were doing flyers for everywhere you could think of and no one else could touch them. They were popular and I became popular by association. Ravers live for the next event – fact. So when you are stood outside a rave with a bunch of flyers, it's obvious that it is vital information and people will be drawn to you.

Being entrepreneurial, I used to get my mates in for free on the condition that they helped hand the flyers out at the end of the night. It really was a tailor-made position for me; if I got ten mates to help out, I could do more flyers. I'd make around a tenner on each, so that was a hundred quid on top of the free night out. Not fucking bad. My mate Chris worked in a sports shop. He let me put flyers in the shop and would supply me with free trainers in return for free nights out – all I had to do was use my loaf and I could get anything I wanted. (When the owner died of a heart attack in the shop itself, it had nothing to do with him finding out I'd been getting freebie trainers. Honest.)

The Flying Squad loved me because with 10 to 15 lads on it I could dish out more paper than anyone else. And as the scene became more commercial, they moved into selling tickets. It was a logical move and it had a knock-on-effect – people knew that I could get them tickets, now, so they started doing flyers for me after their night out as well so my little empire was expanding. My makeshift plan seemed to be working. Whatever that plan was. So far it had only consisted of getting in on the scene and making money from it.

Girls were finding me a lot more attractive than they'd ever done before, too. My second brush with the long arm of the law happened when I was around 19 or 20. I'd smashed up my first car – a Ford Capri, which I absolutely loved – and had been reduced to buying myself an Austin Allegro, a gold, two-door estate. Three hundred quid, it cost: it wasn't much to look at but it got me from A to B and lasted me a year. I'd met some young bird from Basingstoke while I was flying a rave – she was fit as fuck, really pretty with massive tits, and all over me like a rash. She just had to have it, but I couldn't take her home because I was still living with my mum. So I took her off to a lonely old country lane in the Turbo Passion Wagon. I had her in the back on her hands and knees and I was banging the fucking daylights out of her when there was a knock on the window. It was the Old Bill; he didn't know whether to stare at her tits or bollock me. Eventually, reluctantly, he decided on the latter.

Can you please move on, sir?

Oh, for fuck's sake, it's a quiet road.

Can you please move on, sir?

So I'm out and zipped up and away, with one very pissed off bird in the back and two very sore balls.

It was always cars, with me, back then.

After the Allegro I got myself a BMW – a white, G-reg 320i. Two and half grand, it cost – I can see it in the garage now. I was in love. I put 500 quid down and had the rest on the strap. I thought I'd made it. I'd been on holiday to Ibiza and on my first day back, there I was, all chilled out, putting flyers in shops and posters in windows – just going about my usual business. As I was getting in to drive to the next shop, a car went past and just missed taking my driver's door off. You can be the nicest, quietest person in the world or someone with the worst attitude – it doesn't matter. When your motor is at risk of being damaged, we all react the same in that situation. He screeched to a halt and reversed back up the road to shout and swear at me, saying what he'd do to me and how lucky I was that he didn't get out of his car. I was filling mine up and couldn't really have a row as I was loaded down with boxes and rolls of posters so I just let him say his piece. Soon as the car was full, I drove after him until he stopped at some traffic lights. Seconds out, round two: His window was already open. 'What did you say to me, wanker?' I asked. What he said was irrelevant; it was how he'd said it. All I cared about was how hard he was getting hit. He looked up just in time to see my fist connect with his face – perfect timing – and I left him sparked out and slumped over the wheel.

That was my third meeting with the police. I begged forgiveness from all concerned and promised that it wouldn't happen again. Which was true. He wasn't going to do anything as stupid as that again, was he? I only ended up getting done for common assault, although I would have thought getting knocked out when you're sat in your car at traffic lights was a pretty fucking uncommon occurrence.

The odd rumble aside, things were on the up and up. I was saving myself money, getting free nights out for me and my mates, building great contacts *and* earning. The Flying Squad didn't have a ticket outlet outside of London until I put it to Russell that they needed a ticket agent, someone who was on the ball, to sell in a place like . . . well, like Camberley, for example. He jumped to his own conclusion – he asked me to be their ticket agent because I was from Camberley and they needed someone like me to operate outside of the capital. He was sharp, I'll give him that.

The deal was, the ticket price was £15 to me and I'd knock them out at £16.50 – a 10% mark-up. The thing was, no one ever bought just one ticket at a time, it was usually in bunches of 10, so I'd get around 15 quid per handover each time. I'd make 50 quid or more in a night and more weeks than not I'd sell out – 300 or 400 tickets, at £1.50 a pop, with my flying money, £200 a week, was adding up nicely. Once it really all clicked, I stopped looking for a 'proper' job. Hmmm . . . four nights a week clubbing and giving out flyers to birds, or 40 hours of working like a dog to make my boss even richer? Not a tough decision. I couldn't even keep a job on the side. I was leading a strange life, compared to most people's, working Thursday to Sunday, travelling round to clubs which were largely in the same area with kicking out times at two, three, four, five and six in the morning, so I could hit them all. I used to go to bed about 8pm and get up at around 1am, drive up to London and be outside a club at 2am. I'd head back home at about seven in the morning for some more well-deserved kip. When I was working those kind of hours, there were no other jobs which could fit around it.

Thanks to a lot of hard work, my sideline had become my main source of income. Being made redundant turned out to have been a great career move.

Before too long, me and my team were outselling everyone else in The Flying Squad by miles. But after six months or so, it all went Pete Tong between me and the Squad, as these things have a habit of doing. More than that actually, it went Annabel Chong . . . *totally* fucked.

It was frustrating and, like most disagreements, it was over money. Me and some mates flew some stuff somewhere and they said they'd only pay a silly amount because there was only a small number of us there. Which was bollocks. I argued and they said that the promoter had checked up on us. Which was even bigger bollocks. They refused to pay. What can you do, eh?

While I'd been happy in my job, it was always in the back of my mind that I'd set my own company up – most people have probably pondered it and it's only the doubts that put the kibosh on it. *What if people don't pay up? What if it takes forever to make any money? What if it all goes tits up?* For some reason, few people seem to ask, *What if I do fuck all with my life working for someone else and later live to regret it when I've got nothing to show for it?* It was time to act. Time to make the dream a reality. I took this as my wake-up call and went for it.

We had a *You'll never work in this town again* falling out and I told them to take the money they owed me, roll it up into a nice little bundle and stick it right up their arses. What's more, I said I was going to set up by myself and that I'd take all their business from them. They said I'd never do it and if I did I wouldn't last more than five minutes on my own.

I walked off into the sunset with the sound of them laughing in the distance. Let them laugh, I thought. I didn't give a shit.

You know when you say something in the heat of the moment and then live to regret it? I'm not talking about *me*, I'm on about The Flying Squad. I proved them wrong on both counts. The very next day, I set up on my own and, just over five minutes later, I had my first contract – one of *their* contracts.

I can't remember who it was now, but the call went something like this.

'Alright? It's Terry. You know, I've been flying your raves for you?'

'Alright, Tel?'

'Good, thanks. Look, I've just left The Flying Squad. I'll be doing your flying myself from now on. Better rates, same service. That alright with you?'

'Fuck, yeah. Nice one, son.'

I rang every one of their clients. A few decided to stay with the Squad for old times' sake or out of loyalty – fair enough, if it ain't broke, don't fix it – but at least 50 per cent of them decided to come with me. They knew me and my mates were shit hot at flyers, and I'd sold a fuck of a lot of tickets by now, and they didn't give a shit about anything else except bodies in their clubs.

They also knew that, unlike a lot of flying teams, we weren't a load of pilled-up chancers. Yes, we were out for a good time but if we said we'd turn up somewhere and fly it we turned up and flew the fucker. They weren't going to find 3,000 flyers chucked in a bin somewhere down the road – not that The Flying Squad did this either.

I undercut The Squad initially, and then brought my prices up once the contracts were solid. Business went from strength to strength, and people started to notice us. I bought fifty bright red MA2 flying jackets with a fuck-off Turbo Promotions logo on the back and smaller one on the left breast pocket and kitted everyone out in them. They were a huge hit. It was my intention to make us stand out from the crowd because you've got to be visible. In order to *be* the business, you have to *look* the business and that's truer in promotion than in anything else. You can't promote other people's events unless you can promote yourself, can you? That was what I kept in mind and it worked – I had the strapline, *Look out for the red jackets – Flying a club near you!* put onto all advertising material and business cards.

It might sound naff to some, but we were passionate about flying – we took it personally if clubs didn't get many in. And our passion stood out. The first thing you noticed was that you'd hear us before you saw us. We were *enthusiastic* about the event whose flyers we were giving out and that gave the thing credibility through our conviction. Most didn't give a shit; they'd just stand handing them out and grunt occasionally. Here's a tip from me: every time someone just gives you a flyer without bothering to tell you what it's for, you just chuck it in the bin without bothering to look at it. We were *active*. We had a selling point and created a buzz. Punters would actually come to us and watch what we were doing, rather than walk past and have a flyer stuffed in their hand. With us you'd be eager to see what we were shouting about, like it was some street theatre performance. That was something I insisted on with my staff – they needed the balls to make a noise and not care if they seemed a bit odd in the process. Because we were all ravers, we were used to being a bit daft and shouting silly things so we were never too embarrassed to shout the name of the club we were promoting.

The second thing you noticed about us was those red jackets. They were so loud; they could compete with the shouting and soon became part of our corporate image. They ended up so popular that I ordered a load more and sold them on. People bought them just to say they were part of the team – that's how mad it all got. Funnily enough, in Camberley, in January 2006, I saw a geezer walking around wearing one of them. It was a funny sight, all those years on: I wish I'd asked to buy it off him because my own have all long gone. The Turbo clothing range was a bit of a laugh really. It made a bit of money, although the idea behind it was to get our name out. That was the priority.

The third thing anyone noticed was the hair. We all had skinheads – people probably thought we were some Neo Nazi group giving out right-wing propaganda leaflets at first. We got some funny looks until they realised who we were. The point is, we looked out of the ordinary and people remembered us.

We also kept a close eye on the competition. To be fair to the Squad, they were good operators but a lot of other little fly-by-night teams would spring up from time to time, take a bit of business here and there and fade away. I watched them all closely. They'd dish their flyers out in little plastic bags from their box and when the box was empty, they'd fuck off. So I made sure that I always had three boxes and would be there long after they had done their thing. I'd call up any promoters we weren't working for and point out that we always bothered to make three boxes up because we weren't a lazy bunch of piss-taking wankers. Lots of times, these other promoters would ask around and end up coming back to me and taking us on.

In the months that followed, there was so much work on offer that I could do all kinds of deals with clubs and promoters. Whether they wanted four different flyers or one, all prices were negotiated and we were all happy. As more work came in, I was able to sit back from flying and let other people work for me. That was a bonus, because there was a lot of work. We'd spend all day phoning round, picking up boxes and doing all the behind-the-scenes stuff that no one ever saw. My organisational skills weren't brilliant then, and I found myself on a wing and a prayer more than once. I'd have scraps of paper everywhere, notes to myself, things to do, people to see, all with no meaning to anyone other than me. Somehow, it was easier to keep track of chaos.

After a year or so, Turbo Promotions had all the clubs in London coming to us. I charged £15 per head and paid my team 10 quid a night, so straight away I was making a fiver on each body. But often they just wanted to get in for free without pay, which was easily arranged; then the whole 15 quid went in my back pocket. By now, I was earning around six hundred quid a week from flyers alone and was also selling tickets and not having to pay for anything when I went out anywhere. It was all very Henry Hill-ish – where he takes his bird out for the first time, getting in free, getting recognition, the best seats, and the VIP treatment. I'd get bottles of champagne brought over and loads of birds wanting to know me. As a teenager, I'd not been that confident around women and now I was shagging different girl every night . . . if it was a blonde with big tits yesterday, it must be a brunette with long legs today. Sometimes, privately, I had to pinch myself. It can go to your head if you're the wrong kind of person. But I didn't have time to let that happen. There was so much going on every day that I couldn't afford to stop and bask in it all. I had to push myself further all the time. You know the saying: no pain, no Merc.

It wasn't all work and no play, though. We'd have a right laugh every night we were flying. Some of the sights we saw emerging from clubs ranged from amazing to ridiculous: there were people who really dressed up for the occasion with face paints and girls dressed so sexily and flamboyantly – the kind who were real exhibitionists and took having fun seriously. Then you'd see geezers who were sweating and gurning with their tops off, wide-eyed and still dancing. They defied all probability – you just couldn't take that many drugs in one go and live. They would come up to us, buzzing their tits off, just to talk so they could carry the night on. We'd always have fun and play a few tricks on them. We'd tell them that, *Her over there really fancies you!* and watch the scene evolve. It was all harmless and part of the whole experience. We knew we could have a laugh with these people because they were a good crowd. There were regulars who we knew from different events and they would always stop for a chat. I'd think, *Fucking hell, this lot go out more often than I do!*

By now, my mum and Nan were working for me and mum's place was looking like a warehouse. Actually, it *was* a warehouse. It was also part doss-house, part call centre, full of boxes and flyers and people crashed out on the sofa. With no overheads, all I had to fork out on was tea bags, Jammy Dodgers, and phone bills. Mum and Nan helped me stuff envelopes and load boxes into the car, so we had a family business on our hands with yours truly as the boss, Don Turbo. Mum loved it, though it was hard graft at times and she probably wouldn't have admitted it back then. I couldn't have managed without them. No way could I have stuffed *10* envelopes on my Jack Jones, let alone 10,000. I'd have felt more like Terry Waite than Terry Turbo, sat in a room all that time alone; it wasn't healthy. And fuck it – that's what family is for – to pitch in, whatever the task. But the way they came in was a Godsend. They helped me build it all up and it was amazing to have their support from the very beginning. Without your mum's support on anything, you're nowhere. I'd trust my mum with my life and her opinion means everything to me. Most geezers would see it as a weakness, being at home and bringing your mum in to work with you. I saw it as strength. She's smart and street-wise and takes shit from no-one. Can't ask for more than that.

The mailouts got absolutely mental once it all kicked off. We'd be sat in the living room, with my auntie Lynne helping out too, surrounded by boxes and piles of flyers. You'd have to crane your neck to speak to anyone and would have to be able to limbo if you wanted a cuppa. Something had to give – it was costing us a fortune in plasters for paper cuts, apart from anything else. In the end, I rented an office – a room in a block in Sandhurst, called Goldenball House, which was funny and, I hoped, a lucky omen – and I took on a dedicated mailing company to do the fliers. I couldn't expect my mum, Nan and auntie to spend the rest of their days stuffing envelopes with paper. It was probably a breach of the Geneva Convention.

As you'd imagine, we had run-ins with other flying teams from time to time. I remember a night at Camden Palace. This bird was off her face and having a go at my staff. Fine – except she was the girlfriend of a rival team's boss and it all related to a fall-out between the pair of us. One of the lads phoned me and let me know what happened. I wasn't happy about it although, in the scheme of things, it was just some drunken bird with a big fat mouth. But if she and her bloke had a problem with us they should have come to me – not the people who worked for me.

A few days later, we were flying a rave for the Orange Organisation on a race track in Essex when I spotted them with a couple of their mates. Time for some payback, I thought. My lads followed me and, with my eyes only on the bird, I told her to lay off abusing my staff. Problems were to be sorted out with me, end of story. Obviously I threw a truck-load of swearing in too, just to prove I knew more naughty words than her.

I targeted her because I wanted her boyfriend to intervene. Sure enough, he couldn't resist it.

'Don't talk to my girlfriend like that,' he said.

He even pushed me. Who the fuck did this prick think he was? Just when I had my excuse, it became obvious why he'd suddenly grown a pair of bollocks. Suddenly, a group of a dozen or more guys appeared behind him – 10 or so doormen and a right pair of right lumps I knew from the scene. Following this guy's heroic one-liner, they surrounded us like a red Indians in a shit western movie. We were outnumbered and going to get a kicking. I told my lot to stand their ground. Although it wasn't their battle, we had to go down fighting, whatever the outcome.

But nothing happened.

Bizarrely, they all dispersed as quickly as they'd arrived. I praised my lads for keeping it together. They were prepared to have a go and none of them was older than 20. I was only 22 myself, for fuck's sake. It was only as we were heading back to the car when one of the doormen asked if we wanted to help clear up after the rave for 30 quid each. Ah . . . confusion over, they hadn't bottled it; they just didn't want to fight in front of witnesses. If we'd stayed and taken them up on their kind offer of earning a bit of extra pocket money, we would have got smashed to bits.

'No thanks,' I said, and we were off.

The lads I had working for me didn't need any aggravation and this business demanded that you looked after the team so they'd look after you. I didn't talk them into a kicking; technically, I'd saved them from one. It isn't worth fighting when you don't have to. Or if you haven't got backup, of course. There's always other days, if need be.

I had a smile on my face as I drove away, though. By now, I was making £40,000 or £50,000 a year on flying and it felt pretty fucking good. In fact, it was abso-fucking-lutely fucking amazing. As fuck. I said I'd do it and I'd done it. There I was, the kid from Camberley who'd proved himself against the odds. I thought back to the way The Flying Squad laughed me out of the door the day I'd quit. They weren't laughing any more. I'd told them they'd rue the day and they were ruing it alright . . . and there was more to be done. I'd been waiting for my time to cut loose and do it my own way. I was the one with the name and the face. (Funnily enough, things are cool between us now – they're good guys and still doing well in the trade.)

All I needed to do was keep my nose clean, and I knew I'd make money.

The only way I could be stopped was by either being killed or put in prison.

THE SCENE

I had been thinking for a while about putting a magazine together, not least of all because it seemed the most obvious idea in the history of obvious ideas.

I knew all the promoters and everyone connected to the scene and had a good reputation that was growing all the time. There was room for a magazine about raving and it would give us something else to offer the promoters we worked for. Pages of listings, happenings, opinions and reviews, people could advertise in it and it would become something all the clubbers would want. You didn't need to go to a club or a record store to find out what events were on – everything you needed would be within the pages.

That wasn't my only motivation.

There was this bloke called Ralph, from Birmingham. He was less than five feet tall, always E-d off his head and he wore this ridiculous beret – imagine Danny DeVito doing an impression of Frank Spencer at a rave, and you'd almost be there. I dunno, something about him was never quite right – for someone so into the scene, he never looked like he belonged. He had a flying company and ticket outlet called Oracle, who joined forces with none other than The Flying Squad to cover most of the country. Ralph and me had what you'd accurately describe as a hate/hate relationship, which could only ever get worse. It didn't intentionally start out that way – it was just me and the lads taking the piss out of his beret every time we saw him, shouting things like 'Power to the people!' from Citizen Smith. For some reason it really got to him. We would probably have stopped and moved on to another target if he hadn't reacted so badly. It's the first rule you learn in school, isn't it? If they're getting to you, don't show it. Perhaps Ralph had never been to school. Anyway, we kept taking the piss and the hatred really started, probably fuelled by and his association with the Flying Squad. He used to slag us off to people and try to rubbish our reputation, so then we'd take the piss more, he'd talk to more people, blah blah blah, until it got ridiculous. One night, one of my mates swiped the beret when he was wearing it and legged it. He came storming up to me, ranting that someone from the Turbo Promotions team had gone too far this time. He demanded it back immediately.

'Ralph,' I said. 'I haven't got a fucking Scooby what you're on about, but what the boys get up to on a night, other than give out flyers, is up to them.'

'Where's my fucking hat?!' he shouted.

'I don't know and I couldn't give a fuck,' I said. 'To be honest, I wouldn't even piss on it if it was on fire.'

This was an unfortunate thing to say because, actually, it was.

Ralph suddenly screamed and pointed behind me. I turned . . . they were all stood behind us in a circle, 10 blokes and five girls, all in Turbo Promotions jackets, dancing round his beret which was well and truly torched, burning away like a sacrifice to the rave gods. I couldn't help but laugh and Ralphy-boy didn't see the funny side.

'That's it!' he snarled.

'Oo-oo-ooh!' was our handbaggily camp reply. He stormed off with us all shouting, 'Hat's it!' to each other.

That's *what* though? Alright, his hat got cremated and we'd had a laugh at his expense. But no one got hurt, so I didn't see it as that much of a problem. I knew I'd have been annoyed, too, but I also knew I'd have seen the funny side of it. There's a lot more problems in the world than a burnt hat.

The next morning, we were outside a club flying when our

mate Ralph came out with some pilled-up retard called Paul, the editor of self-styled 'controversial dance magazine', *Eternity*. Both were bouncing around with glow sticks, tops off, stinking of Vicks Vapour Rub, gurning away like the biggest rave cliché you can imagine. I couldn't resist another wind up.

'Where's your hat, Wolfie?' I asked, with a boyish giggle. He told me to fuck off and Paul stepped in with, 'Do you know who I am?'

'You're a fucking idiot, that's who you are.' I said. 'Now put your top back on before you catch cold. Before you *really* need some Vicks.'

'I'm the editor of *Eternity*,' he said, bouncing around in my face.

I don't know why he told me or how he thought I'd react.

'I don't care if you're the editor of the *News of the World*,' I said. 'But one thing's for sure . . . you really *are* a fucking idiot. If you're a magazine editor, what are you doing getting off your face in a club?'

'I'm gonna destroy you,' he started saying. 'I'm going to finish you and your business.'

These were very bold words, but words I'd heard too many times already and, to be honest, I find idle threats a bit boring.

'Look,' I said. 'If you want a row, I'll smash you and this other cunt up and we can all go home. Otherwise, piss off.'

They pissed off and I forgot about the whole incident until a good mate of mine, Murray Beetson who owned Dreamscape, phoned me up a month or two later.

'You want to get your hands on *Eternity* magazine's latest edition, Terry,' he said. 'There's something in there you should see. You won't believe it even after you've read it.'

I was intrigued, so I jumped in the motor and spent the next six hours driving around looking for a copy in a newsagents. Fucking typical, I found the award-winning magazine in a poky little shop on the outskirts of nowhere, after almost a full tank of petrol. I chuckled at the irony . . . the dance music bible not stocked in any major newsagent, but out in the sticks, in a local shop for local ravers.

Sitting in the car, I opened it and started at the beginning, with the editorial. I couldn't make any sense of it at all: he was trying to be all abstract and New Agey, in a post-modernist, up-your-own-arse sort of style. This lasted for two pages and was the biggest pile of pretentious bollocks I'd ever read. By the time I got to the end, I wasn't sure whether I was being insulted or not. That all changed when I flicked through to the centre pages.

Fucking hell! The centre spread was a double-page hatchet job on me and Turbo Promotions. It was a no-holds-barred attack. Murray was right – I couldn't believe my eyes. I was absolutely fuming. It said I was a disgrace to the rave scene, a hooligan, I was doing everything the wrong way, and that promoters shouldn't let people like me hand flyers out.

People like me? I was a raver to the soles of my feet. I loved the scene, and if I'd not been in it business-wise I'd have been in there with my whistle and my Vicks myself. Granted, we all had skinheads and we looked a bit scary but we were totally professional, we provided a good service and he had fuck all right or reason to call me a hooligan or cast aspersions on my business methods. Apart from anything else, him and his little Brummie mate were the ones always fucked-up on drugs at every event.

I phoned a few promoters and asked them what it was all about, and to get their opinions. They all said pretty much the same thing: they thought whoever wrote it was as mad as a bag of snakes. Phew, so it wasn't just me.

So I called Paul up, and let him and Ralph know that if I ever saw either of them again, they would be likely to have a serious accident. That was it – they'd pushed me too far and I was prepared to smash them up to prove they couldn't go around pulling such shit. My blood was really boiling.

A few days later I got a letter from them saying they'd told the police and had taped the threatening phone call, so if anything *did* happen to them the coppers knew all about my threat. I backed off, calmed down and took the proverbial chill pill. I probably wouldn't have done them anyway; I'd already vented my anger. The fact that they'd bricked it and gone to the Old Bill was good enough for me. They'd always be watching their backs in future, too – a nice little bit of mental torture to throw into the mix.

Murray advised me to leave it there. 'Keep doing what you're doing because they are only jealous of you,' he said. 'That's the best way of fighting back.'

Those were wise words, and they were the final push I needed to start my own magazine. If those two clowns could run one, I was certain I could. I sat down and thought it through properly – deciding on the amount of time and money available to put it together and how much I'd need to take in order for it to earn money. With an idea of page numbers and dimensions, I was able to work out how many adverts could go in and how much there was to be made. I rang around and asked if people would be interested in advertising and most of them said yes. It seemed viable. I double-checked. It still seemed viable.

I set to work on it. The result was *The Scene* magazine – another venture that started out relatively small, but with big plans. First up, it was an A5-sized full-colour magazine featuring listings, regular features, reviews and interviews. If I say it myself, it was a good read. Meanwhile, things could only get better – a lot fucking better. I heard a rumour that *Eternity Magazine* was getting into financial trouble. It happened a lot back in those days – after all, the rave scene was still, largely, an industry populated by kids without much of a business background and lots of people got burned and went under. Some fought their way back and had another go (and sometimes another and another) and some sank without trace. It was all part of the learning curve. Anyway, sure enough, the magazine folded soon after that. I remember mates of mine coming on the phone, pissed off that it had gone bust owing them money. Like I say, it happens, and nowadays, I'd probably be a lot more sympathetic to *Eternity*'s plight. I'm not saying I'd help them out, mind you – I'd still have a good laugh to myself and probably knock the top of a bottle of shampoo. Back then, though, I absolutely loved it. At *The Scene* we couldn't let it pass without giving it a special mention. We set up the Eternity Magazine Memorial Fund and ran a poignant leader: *It is with great sadness that we have to bring all* The Scene *readers some very disturbing news. Eternity magazine has now become a thing of the past. They have gone bust owing £250,000. Here at* The Scene *we feel that without* Eternity *magazine, the rave scene will fall apart. Just think of all the poor ravers that used to read the introduction and think, 'What the fuck are they on about?'*

Fuck 'em. If we could wind them up even more, then I was a happier man. The Scene was all about taking the piss. It had silly articles and jokes and was never intended to be anything you'd take seriously. I never set out to produce a 'controversial dance magazine' – nothing as grandiose as that. It was just a pocket-sized mag that would give people a laugh but would also keep them up to date on all the happenings in rave world.

It ran for quite some time and became very popular. As it took off, it helped me fund other projects and ran parallel with my events when I went into promoting. When One Nation was eventually set up, *The Scene* was synonymous with it and they were a good combination because, with raves being a monthly thing to begin with, I could concentrate on the magazine in my spare time. Assuming I ever had any. Having both of them running gave me the foothold I'd been looking for – it was a good move, establishing my name and status *before* promoting. Going from Turbo Promotions to *The Scene* and then One Nation would give me quite a powerful position – people saw me as a driving force and took notice of what I was doing.

I had my mum in the magazine with a regular feature as Auntie

Trisha – a mental agony aunt who just talked a load of bollocks. We used to get people to write in and the maddest letter we received won an *Auntie Trisha solved my Problem* t-shirt. We'd have letters like this:

Dear Auntie Trisha
My mother in law was a witch! She lived with me and my wife. She nagged and moaned at me constantly for the 20 years she lived with us. She never let me watch football or action films, she made me do the washing up every night and take the dog out. Everything I did was wrong and she thought she was always right. Eventually I couldn't take any more, so I killed her, hacked up her body, put it in a bin liner and threw it in the Thames. Do you think I over-reacted?

That one was sent in by someone calling himself Mr N Bates. It was this kind of silliness that I loved and encouraged. We also had Gurner of the Month which was always a crowd-pleaser – people sent in photos of their mates when they were absolutely mashed and we'd print them. It was so funny – I even had a few of me in there. My favourites were when someone had fallen asleep and pissed themselves, and their 'mates' would put them in mad positions, dress them up, put make up on them, shave something off – they always had me laughing like a lunatic. We had another column called *Mystic Peg, she's off her head*, which was a pastiche of that bird off the lottery programme. It was a horoscope column where she just spurted a load of complete and utter nonsense.

There were regular columns from DJs and MCs, interviews and reviews of all the latest events. I liked to add articles that were about nothing at all – so you'd get to the end of it and wonder why the fuck you'd just wasted five minutes reading it. I think the humour was quite a reaction to Ralph and Paul's self-indulgent drivel. Pointless humour makes you laugh, whereas pointless pretension just bores you rigid. People wanted to be entertained and I wanted a magazine that could make people laugh instead of feel patronised and alienated.

Danielle and Rochelle, two DJs, worked for me on the magazine. They'd write articles on up and coming acts and interview anyone in the club and music scene they wanted to. As editor, I'd OK everything before they did it and see if it was worthy of publication – really just to make sure they were on the right lines, which they always were. It helped that they were already on the scene and knew what they were talking about.

One of the best things about *The Scene* was our legendary trips abroad.

With Britain being the birthplace of raving, lots of promoters would get called up and asked to fly off somewhere and sprinkle a little of their magic on some foreign club. With the flying and the tickets and now *The Scene* going strong, we'd often get invited along. The promoter would just add a few of us to his entourage, the foreigners would pick up the bill and we'd print a nice big feature about the event when we got home – a win-win-win scenario. We went all over the place: Canada, Switzerland, Tenerife, Ibiza and Ayia Napa, to name just a few. My mate Chris Brown had recently set up United Dance. Within no time, they were huge, mainly because of Chris's commitment to the scene. He knew what he was doing – he wasn't one of these cowboys who wanted to bleed the scene dry in a year and then fuck off, he was in it because he loved it and was keen to see it evolve. After battling the council to get a licence, he started out at the Stevenage Arts and Leisure Centre – a 3,000 capacity gig – and later he merged with Temptation before setting up home in Bagleys. I remember a trip to Canada with United Dance. We flew from Gatwick, upset a few passengers on the way and touched down in Toronto ready for action. It was fucking mental. There was me, Chris Brown, Slipmatt, Bradley Carter, Gabby, Maxine, Bolino, Dougal, Vinylgroover, DJ Sy and Ellis D. We were met off the plane by our hosts, Mark and Shannon. They already knew what to expect and I think we exceeded their expectations within the first minute of meeting them. Once outside the airport, there was a massive stretch limo waiting for someone. Joking, I hatched a plan to hijack the thing by acting as though it was for us and we knew about it. We marched over and told the driver to start loading our bags into the boot and to make it snappy.

OK then, 'Put them in the fucking *trunk* . . . and make it snappy.' For fuck's sake.

Mark and Shannon tried to intervene, but we kept talking over the top of them and shushing – we knew what we were doing, we had it all under control. With the trunk loaded up, we instructed him to take us to the finest hotel in all the land. He looked over to Mark as if to say, *Who the fuck are these English loonies?*

Mark just shrugged and opened the door for us, 'Come on. Get in. We're going to the Days Inn, probably not the finest, but still pretty good.'

We all paused for a second as it dawned on us – the limo really *was* for us. I could hardly believe it. And the shame of it hushed us until the first bottle of bubbly was popped. The limo was like a nightclub on wheels; huge and luxurious, top of the range, five stars, no expense spared, VIP treatment. Everything we wanted was in there waiting for us . . . pizza, vodka, beer, champagne, more pizza, more beer, more vodka . . . the lot. One of the lads wanted a bit of puff, so Mark delved into a bag and pulled out an ounce. No questions asked. The Canadians really knew how to treat their guests. I apologised for our silly behaviour and just played it down like we knew the limo was for us in the first place . . . and boy, were we grateful. It was the best greeting we could have hoped for.

It was easy to forget why we were there. Looking out the window, there was Toronto whizzing past and we were in a limo being paid for by someone who paid to fly us all out there to have fun. Don't forget, I'm just a geezer from the Old Dean who'd been made redundant from a job selling scaffolding a year or so earlier. If I'd have thought too hard about the situation, it would have been too humbling and I'd have ended up behaving myself. I had to enjoy the moment. Supposedly, we were there to promote and put our faces to raves, but our main plan was to have a good time and bag as many freebies as possible. Half-cut and no doubt jet-lagged, we dropped our cases off at the hotel and went straight out to see what was happening.

The club promoter sent a bird called Jennifer to the hotel to look after us and make sure we didn't get lost or arrested before the event. She took us round all the touristy places and to all the best shops to stock up on some designer gear. Shopping was amazing because over there, everything was less than half price. It was a bit embarrassing really because you'd feel guilty, like you were stealing from them. A £50 t-shirt in the UK could be picked up in Toronto for around £20 – back home, you couldn't even pick up moody gear for those prices. Once we discovered the Tommy Hilfiger shop, we practically cleaned it out. It was like Mr Hilfiger himself had puked all over us – we were covered from head to toe. We must have looked like a bunch of women on day one of the January sales.

The rave itself was fantastic – held in a fuck-off warehouse, absolutely packed with thousands of people, all off their nuts. I wasn't too sure what to expect but it was just like going to an English rave but without all the muggers and dickheads. Everyone was up for a good night out and the atmosphere was indescribable, like the whole of Toronto's party people had turned up to see us, all dressed to impress. As we arrived, armed with our boxes of records, all these punters came up to us to take our photos and get our autographs. A large number of very fucking fit young Canadian women got the arses banged off them in the bogs – they were queuing up for it – and we were also kept well supplied with champagne and drugs. Some geezer who was an associate of the promoter came over with a record bag full of Es – there must have been 5,000 pills in there.

He opened his bag up and said, 'Grab some.'

We asked how much they were.

'You're with me, man,' he said. 'Don't be stoopid.' So we weren't. Well, we were. You know what I mean.

We stayed there until 6.30am, called the limo and got pissed on the way back to the hotel. Where we found Slipmatt – who'd snuck out earlier, in bed with a couple of naked birds. The Godfather of Hardcore had been partying hard and he was now fast asleep, as were the two women. But he'd obviously gone first – they'd covered him in green nail varnish, lipstick, eye shadow and some nice looking home-drawn tattoos. There was a smiley drawn on his face and *United Dance in Canada* scrawled across his side. Concerned for him, we did what any mates would do – we took photos.

The next day saw some rather green faces emerge from our rooms. None greener than Slipmatt's boat. He also discovered a pile of light bulbs next to his bed that he'd nicked in his drunken state, leaving a trail of darkness through the hotel to his room. After some more sight-seeing and 20 gallons of water each, we went clubbing at The Industry, got pissed up on some really strong cider and ended up tripping our tits off. By accident. Honest. Our 'tourist guide' asked me and Matt if we wanted some mushroom tea. You know what the English are like for drinking tea . . . we thought this was just some hippy-herbal-shit – not actual magic mushrooms. Half an hour later, we were roaming the streets, on trams, buzzing like fuck trying to find something to do.

The day before we left, one of the lads ended up banging this bird who, to put it bluntly, was a fucking skag-head. He was married, which was bad enough, but I was there to work and play, not to be a marriage counsellor. I just told him to use protection if he was going to shag a heroin addict and left it at that. It's not like he'd shag a junkie at home, so fuck knows why he wanted to shag one just because she had a different accent. He told me he did it without a condom and I told him he was fucking stupid. But as boys do, we took the piss out of him. In *Eastenders* at the time, Mark Fowler had HIV and it was a big part of the storyline . . . so from then on, my nameless friend was known as Mark Fowler. It wasn't till the flight home, that the shit hit his fan. He started complaining that his cock was on fire and his bollocks were going to explode. I'm not kidding, I was crying with laughter. Turned out he'd caught his nuts on something when he was banging her – so it wasn't the pox after all. Fuck knows if he ever told his wife.

There was another night of clubbing the following night, but it was my turn to be the lightweight of the group. I turned in early, only to be woken up at six in the morning with 12 geezers jumping up and down on my bed. It was annoying but it just meant that I got up and joined in the party, and could then annoy them when they eventually burnt out.

Once they crashed out, I sneaked out of the room, went to the shops and bought tons, almost literally, of fruit and veg. I borrowed a table from reception and set up a market stall outside the room . . . it was all set out perfectly. I went back in and dragged the others outside. As soon as they clapped eyes on my pitch, they pissed themselves. I borrowed a bumbag from someone to wear so I looked like an authentic market stall holder and we started shouting things like, 'Get your oranges! Five for a pound!' Some of the people staying in the hotel even stopped to buy some fruit.

We'd started losing it a bit, with all the drugs, the booze and no sleep. I remember Ellis D somehow got himself into another dimension where he started thinking he was James Bond. He walked everywhere with an imaginary gun, pulling 007 poses. The Canadians were like, *who is this crazy Englishman?* We smashed our hotel rooms up, like we were in The Who or something, and ordered huge meals – steaks, pizzas, wine – on room service, and hardly even touched them.

Towards the end of our stay, it all went tits up. The guys told Chris that he owed them around three grand for all the 'extras' we had. That was a lot of money, especially ten years ago or more.

'What do you mean, three fucking grand?' he asked.

It turned out they wanted wedging up for all the Es and the puff and the champagne. Because Chris was the promoter behind it, they went to him for the money, but they picked on the wrong guy.

OK, everyone had been taking liberties and necking as many drugs as possible, smashing rooms up, on the take for the whole week and it had mounted up. But fuck that – we'd been told it was free. Now it seemed that *'all expenses included'* means you can have anything you want, but you pay for it. We told them in no uncertain terms that we weren't paying and they stormed off, angry and threatening. We made some enquiries and it turned out that these geezers were connected to a very serious family, if you know what I mean. I emphasise the words *connected* and *family*.

Being in a foreign country and upsetting those kind of people is the last thing anyone wants to do. It wasn't like we could just get on the blower to my mates and ask them to help out. With some big time geezers breathing down our necks for three grand and us being in an unfamiliar country, we did what any other normal human being would do. We went down the road to the martial arts shop and got tooled up with swords and sticks and daggers. Then we called in at the hardware emporium and bought a load of screwdrivers and axes. Fuck it. We'd go down fighting. All of us were completely ninja-d up.

I seriously though it was going to come to that, too, and I don't mind admitting I was fucking worried. These guys had guns, after all; they weren't just going to have a roll around on the floor with us. I didn't relax until we'd gone through check-in at the airport but in the end we managed to flee the country without having to pull any *Kill Bill* shit. Word had got back to England before we did – as soon as we touched down, there were calls from people wanting to know what we'd done. Apparently we'd upset the entire Canadian rave scene and their financial backers.

Interestingly, the main geezer was found dead at the end of a rope a few months after our visit. He'd borrowed a lot of money to put the party on and couldn't pay it back. Whether he hanged himself, or someone else did it for him, it was a horrible way to go. If it *was* the result of him crossing his friends, we could have ended up the same way. Close call.

Soon as we got home, we were airborne again, heading for Ibiza with M8 magazine, United Dance and the Drome club from Birkenhead. It was fucking awesome – nine days of mentalism. There was the M8 night with DJs Joe Deacon and George Bowie, QFX, Bass Instinct, Mikey B, Tizer and a bird from Hamburg called DJ Miss Nic. The Scene had our own night with Slipmatt, Dougal, Brisk, Vinylgroover and MC MC, The Drome had DJ Trix, Christian and MC Cyanide and a German DJ called Westbam. United Dance had every DJ perform on one night and M8 hosted a scratch DJ competition. The last night was set aside for the Club Kaos resident DJs to have a go.

The usual silliness happened. We were drinking all kinds of mad cocktails and getting into scrapes every day and night. We really were the typical daft English lads abroad; the difference was that we got VIP treatment everywhere we went. We took the piss out of the kind hospitality again – vowing that this would be the last time, so we may as well go all out stupid. You only live once.

The girls were mad for it – we shagged anything that moved, sometimes two or three at a time – and we drank gallons of champagne, bottles of spirits and generally had the most degenerate, wasted week and a bit of our lives.

As The Scene grew – it went from a 12 page, black and white skeleton into a full colour, 128 pager with UK-wide distribution – I started thinking more and more about promoting. I knew I had all the tools now – I could flyer, sell tickets, promote it in the mag, I had contacts with DJs and MCs, I knew hundreds of ravers . . .

What was I waiting for?

ONE NATION – THE EARLY DAYS

Well, it ain't that fucking easy.

Yes, I had all the tools to get it up and going. OK, I was a novice and I didn't have the know-how, but if you've got the drive and ambition to set yourself off, the rest usually falls into place. You need to believe in yourself and push yourself constantly and this was where I gave myself another push and got my arse into gear.

There was just one problem: running big events costs a lot of bread and there's a risk you can lose it all. I had no capital to put in and no business plan so it was pointless going to the bank for a loan.

But Lady Luck was looking down on me again. In mid-1993, I got together with a couple of geezers called Andy and Mark, who had a little pirate radio station. Andy was a geezer on my old estate and Mark was just out of nick for ringing cars. They were keen to get into rave promoting and they asked me to get involved. They said they'd bankroll the whole project and gave me free rein to do whatever I thought was right. When you're offered an opportunity like that, you have to take it. We were all taking a risk – I had no real track record and they were investing ten or fifteen grand.

I needed a name . . . something that would sum up my experience of the scene. I was listening to that old Funkadelic song 'One Nation Under A Groove' when it suddenly hit me: One Nation. Perfect! That was how it was born.

For the flyers, I called in a designer called Junior.

'Create something showing people with candles on their heads,' I said. Where the inspiration came from, I have no idea; I just wanted to have something off the wall and freaky to grab people's attention. I'm sure it did: the flyers looked fucking brilliant.

The first One Nation was at the Roller Express in Edmonton on the 11th of December, 1993. It isn't the best area of London but it was a decent venue: the legal capacity was around 2,600, but you could get 3,500 or even 4,000 in there, easy. I copied a few other people's ideas at first, putting together some lights and sound and getting a decent DJ line-up, playing a mix of hardcore and drum'n'bass. Then I worked my arse off flyering it for a couple of months. There was a lot of nerves – how will it go, will there be any problems, will people have a good time and want to come back . . . We charged £12 advance and £20 on the door and I remember walking around, almost in a daze: I didn't know whether to dance or do what. We ended up having around 1,100 in, which was basically around the break-even point. It wasn't great but it was a start.

Our second event, same place, was a sell out, so we made some profit, but not as much as we should have done because we got ripped off in the cash box. I was on the stage MCing and the other partners were supposed to be looking after the money and making sure it was all coming in. But Andy was rolling around on a handful of Es gurning his head off and Mark was on the stage drinking beer and trying to impress a load of birds with his Peter Stringfellow act. So, hang about . . . who the fuck was in the cash box?

I asked Mark. 'It's cool, mate,' he said. 'The venue have got the cash box sorted.' We knew the guy they'd stuck in there.

Oh, well if he's in there then . . . hang on, if he is in the cash box, then we're fucked. Everyone and their granny knew this guy and knew he had sticky fingers. He was a nice guy, in his way, a weaselly little fucker with messy hair like a white afro, but he couldn't keep his hands to himself. It wasn't just us: I was there one night at someone else's event, and the promoter ended up punching his teeth in. *Everyone* said he was on the take, don't let him touch the dough. So we were warned. Sure enough, we came up short when the money was counted. I had a fair idea where it was but I could prove fuck all. That was a big warning bell for me: with Mark and Andy, there was no organisation or control. What's the point in setting something up, getting off your tits and then trusting a thief to handle your money?

We ran a third event there as a May Day Night party and did OK but we weren't setting clubland alight.

After that one, Mark decided he could do a better job organisationally than me. He said he wanted more of a hands-on role, and it was his cash so I couldn't really argue.

Right from the off, the omens for the fourth night weren't good. His flyers looked like your granny had done them with a Letraset kit. He picked all the DJs himself – just people he liked, including at least one girl DJ he was desperate to bone – and paid no attention to what the punters liked. Also, like the Einstein he was, he put the event on on the same night as Elevation. Elevation was the biggest event in London at that time, so this was commercial suicide.

Predictably, the party was shit and we lost money. Worst of all, it was still under the One Nation name, which I didn't like. It was my name, after all, and now I was handing it over to this guy for him to make a mess of.

I said I'd do the next event, but Mark was adamant he'd do it his way again. I was going to walk away at this point but morbid curiosity kept me with them.

He hadn't learned his lesson. He arranged the next party for the week after a Bank Holiday, when everyone had spent their money and wouldn't be going out for a bit. I couldn't decide if he was a bit mental or just absolutely stupid. It would have been a brave thing to take on a big event – if he was aware of it – but doing something straight after a Bank Holiday was the most dim-witted decision I'd ever heard. You've heard of the X Factor; this was the Y Factor . . . why the fuck would anyone do such a thing?

He just wasn't switched on to what was happening, so he waded in without a clue and lost money each time. There he was scratching his head, wondering why, and he couldn't see any of it.

Rule Number Fucking One: Whoever you are, you cannot promote a rave unless you are passionate and knowledgeable about the scene. And if you're one step down from a village idiot, you certainly can't. To adapt a well-known phrase, he couldn't organise a rave in a dance club.

All he wanted was to make money, and the same went for Andy.

There's only so much fucking everything up that even really dense people can take before they work out that they're not cut out for something and eventually they realised they were in the wrong game.

They called a meeting.

'We want to call it a day,' said Mark.

Thank fuck for that – if they'd carried on as they were, we'd be more in debt than Ethiopia.

'OK chaps,' I said, all amicable. 'I understand your position. I'm gonna carry on with One Nation on my own, then.'

'No you're fucking not,' said Mark. 'If you want to carry on you can buy the business off me.'

'Buy *what* fucking business off you?' I said. 'You've run a few shit events, which got shitter after you asked me to step aside. There's nothing to buy.'

It degenerated into a big row. He was adamant I couldn't just go away and run One Nation events on my own. I was adamant he was a cunt, and I could, and I was.

'First, you took me off what I was doing,' I said. 'You got me into this promoting. Now you don't want to do it, that's fine. Second, One Nation is my fucking brand name, not yours. So bollocks to you. I'm going it alone, and if I'm going to fund it and do it myself, what's it to you?'

They weren't having it, so I laid it on the line. 'Look,' I said. 'We can either do this like adults, or we can sort it out the naughty way. You get whoever you want to get, and I'll get whoever I want to get, and we'll meet up somewhere and have it out with machetes. Whoever's still standing at the end keeps One Nation.'

I was bluffing, but they didn't call me. I walked away, grinning and whistling to myself. Funnily enough, I bumped into Andy three or four years ago. He said, 'You must owe us some money for One Nation?'

I said, 'You fucking prick . . . you used to sit in the corner, off your nut. Mark put the money up but did fuck all else. I did all the work and, yeah, I've made money. But I've lost money too. Whatever I've done, I've done it all myself. Fuck off.'

It had all been a bit of a disaster in one way, but in another it had been a great experience. I'd learned a lot of lessons and made a lot of mistakes at Mark's expense.

First off, the fucking cashbox. I said, THE FUCKING CASHBOX! Repeat 1,000 times till it's in your thick skull. That is the Golden Rule. Always, ALWAYS, have someone in there. Never let anyone you can't trust with your life take your money for you.

Second, Dates. Don't try to go up against the biggest people in town and don't try to run events when everyone's pissed their last penny piece up the wall.

Third, Organisation. Plan, plan, plan. Know exactly how much you're going to spend and what you're going to spend it on, and exactly how many people you need in to break even.

Fourth, The Event. It's no fucking good relying on the club's lights and getting one poxy laser in. Your light show doesn't have to be a religious experience, but you need smoke, lots of lasers and lots of extra lights. People need to know they're at a party. Same goes for the sound system: bring your own bass bins and decks if you're not sure the club can give you what you need.

Fifth, DJs. Don't book a load of idiots just because they're your mates – or women DJs just because they've got nice arses and you want to shag them. Book DJs the punters want to hear.

Last, but not least: Naughtiness. Free ecstasy and speed, limitless booze and underdressed birds will be everywhere. Remember, you're the fucking promoter now, not a punter. I'd be lying if I said that, in the early days, I didn't bend a few nubile blondes over in the bogs and give them a good seeing-to. Or take a blow job here and there. It was part of being the boss: some beautiful young girl comes up to you, with cleavage everywhere, and whispers in your ear that she swallows and she'd like to see you out back, what are you going to do? But if I was going to do this professionally, I had to cut down on that. After seeing Andy in action, I had to forget all about E. And booze was a no-no, too. This was work.

All good stuff. The only problem was, I *still* didn't have the capital needed to run events on my own. Turbo Promotions was going from strength to strength, and I was making more money from that than I did from any four of my old jobs put together. But it's one thing having a nice regular income: it's another having the wedge needed to slap down on a table and put on a big party.

I got lucky again in 1994. Some friends of mine, John and Andrew Searchfield, bought a Shaz and Tracey nightclub in the centre of Aldershot, kitted it out and renamed it The Rhythm Station. They got a late licence – it was the only rave club in the Thames Valley which stayed open until six in the morning – and they asked me to come on board and promote there. It was the perfect place to make my mark and travel a bit further along the learning curve. First up, I ran a regular Jungle night; it was fucking awesome. Everyone who was into Jungle will remember it – I had Fabio, Grooverider, Mickey Finn, and Top Buzz, real top of the ladder DJs, and Fabio and Grooverider would always be plugging it on their Radio One show. It was a coup to get such a line-up together and dancers came from a long way away. The club only held 1,000 people but the atmosphere was among the best I've ever experienced. Jungle had spun out of the

London clubs a couple of years earlier as a reaction to the commercialisation of rave music; they took the tempo from 120bpm to 145bpm and their influences from Ragga rather than House. Eventually, it diversified into Drum and Bass as we know it today but back then it was massive.

With the Searchfields happy to pay the bills, I was able to plan the events just how I wanted them.

For a while, it ran like a dream and one reason it worked so well was that, unlike a lot of other, fly-by-night promoters of the time, I really gave a shit about giving punters the best night I possibly could. The biggest hurdle in starting a club is building up a following and a reputation – once punters buy into that, then you're on the right road. I was filling the place by delivering the best service I could every week.

We had some great nights. Although I was the promoter, a lot of the hassle and pressure running of the event itself was down to the club. My deal was, I made £1 per head. All I needed to do was have a guy on the door with a clicker – not that I didn't trust John and Andrew, it was just something I had to do after the second night at Roller Express. I didn't need to collect my money till the Monday, so I could drop my guard and relax and have a real piss up every Friday and Saturday night. I used to get free drinks so I'd have a few mates in and between us we'd neck a bottle of Morgans rum, strong stuff which knocked my head off, while we fucked around behind the decks and annoyed people. One night, fed up with me behaving like a drunken arsehole, someone spiked my drink. One minute everything's OK, next it's all going very funny. I walked outside, sat in the car and started throwing up. People were pulling up in the carpark and going, 'Hello, Tel!' and walking off, shaking their heads. They must have thought I was a right fucking degenerate; I'm the promoter and here I am, smashed to pieces and hacking my guts up.

I came back in and sat at the back, groaning. I remember DJ Swift, a big black guy, just taking the piss. 'Can't hold your drink, Tel?'

'Fuck off . . . I'll never book you again!'

'Ha, ha, ha!'

We were rammed full every weekend but it's hard to sustain that level of interest in *anything* and club-goers are a particularly fickle bunch. You go to the same club all the time and, sooner or later, you'll want to go somewhere else. Eventually, it died off – we were getting 300 or 400 people in, which wasn't enough – and I had a meeting with John and Andrew. They went, 'Look, Tel, we're paying for the flyers and stuff, we're losing money, we can't carry on. We need to bring money in so we're going to have to hire the club out to other promoters.'

That made sense: they could make money from the hire and still take all the proceeds from the bar on top.

As more promoters came in, they elbowed me out of the picture. I wasn't bitter – they were as loyal as they could have been and had kept me there as long as they could. We all have to earn money, so I could understand their decision with no hard feelings. They carried on for a few years, doing really well for themselves, until the police found drugs were being sold there and they got stopped from doing raves. Nothing to do with John and Andrew – they just owned the club and had no idea about the dealing. But that was that – they eventually refurbed it back to a Shaz and Tracie club, called Cheeks.

I owe them a lot. Without them there would have been no club One Nation. They backed me when I had no money and I'll always be grateful to them.

I had one early go on my own. I got involved with this fat bastard from South London who said he'd let me have a club in the West End , really cheap. Only problem was, the club would only let me sell a certain amount of tickets upfront and he'd sell the rest on the door. Plus I couldn't take my own security firm in and I couldn't have anyone in the cash box – this guy would handle all that. Looking back, it couldn't have been any more obvious – he may as well have been wearing a stocking over his head and carrying a sack with 'swag' written on it. But I either went with his terms or I didn't have an event, and I was desperate to get a solo gig under my belt.

Remember my Six Rules from earlier on? Now I had a Seventh: Tickets. By selling the majority on the door, he was able to re-use them and let people in through the back doors when the rave was in full swing. It was a good night, atmosphere-wise, but there was more skimming going on than a squad of plasterers. Fucking hell – he took me for four or five grand and there wasn't much I could do about it. In accepting Fatty's 'deal', I effectively allowed his bird from the cash box to take the tickets and recycle them out to the doormen who re-sold them outside. There was still the right number of tickets behind the desk at the end of the night. Piece of piss, and I had no way of checking up.

I'd worked my nuts off, filled the club to capacity (and beyond, as it turned out). They'd got all the bar takings, the money I paid for venue hire and they still felt obliged to shaft me.

I confronted the guy. I said, 'You're a fucking cunt! You've ripped me off!'

He was all calm, with his door team behind him. 'Don't fucking accuse me,' he said. 'Where's your proof?'

He was right. I hadn't got any.

I said, 'I know you've ripped me off, you can look me in the eyes and shake my hand but I'll never work with you again.'

And I stormed off. I was pretty fucking low about that night, but I was still learning, and one good thing did come out of it. I realised there was a good chance of making moody money if you sidestepped the venue management and went for the head doorman. The venue has its licence on the line and is usually going to be pretty careful about numbers. The door team, on the other hand, were a different kettle of fish. They'd let another 500 extra in for five hundred quid. If the tickets are £20 a pop, that's £9,500 you've just made yourself.

I still couldn't get out of my Catch 22 situation: I wanted to promote but I didn't have the money.

All I could do was to keep asking people to invest. I was out doing flyers and I met up with a couple of geezers, Phil and Mick. Mick was a small bloke with receding hair, an Irish fella, and Phil was short and stout with a ponytail. They seemed like good guys – they ran Desire, when they weren't getting into rucks following Spurs, and they were into making money. In an industry that was still pretty much finding its feet, everyone was. I told them I had no dough but a headful of ideas and needed someone to back me. They said they'd come on board and we'd split the money down the middle. Great.

As it happened, we only did one party together, at The Rocket on the Holloway Road just up from Islington. It was a small thing, around 2,000 people there, but it should have been a great night. The problem was, I'd immediately forgotten Terry's Golden Rule. CASHBOX, Tel, CASHBOX.

They handled the cash box and, at the end of the night, it was light. Very light.

Again, it was a simple enough scam. They had a geezer clicking everyone in on the door, and he must have been a bit forgetful. Surprise, surprise, it turned out he'd clicked through a lot fewer people than my mate, who'd been doing the same thing on the quiet for me. I don't know what it is with people. We'd had an OK night, it would have been something to build on, we could have gone on to great things together maybe. Who knows? But they'd fucked that for the sake of two or three grand. Even more annoying, when it came to divvying up the money they'd already skimmed, Phil said, 'Here's your third, Tel.'

I said, 'Hang about . . . what third? I want half, like we agreed.'

We had the usual confrontation, with discussions about baseball bats and shooters, and said our goodbyes. It wasn't worth arguing about, much less killing or being killed over.

Still, I learned yet another important lesson: when you're in a cash business that teeters on the edge of illegality, with drugs and violence in the air, it is going to be full of cunts. You cannot trust *anyone* except very close friends and your immediate family.

From now on, I was going to do this thing on my own, or not do it at all.

One other good thing came out of the shenanigans at The Rocket: I *had* made a few thousand quid. It wasn't a fortune but it was a start.

I was on the way to launching One Nation as a true business.

UP AND RUNNING

I'd vowed to myself that I wouldn't make any more silly mistakes. I had my set of rules – I forget how many, but there were a lot of them – and I'd made a few mistakes of my own, and watched myself get sucked into a few made by other people.

I sat at home, with the small pile of cash I'd made out of The Rocket, and thought about the way forward. I could add a bit I'd saved up – I'd been earning over five hundred a week on average and had started putting a bit aside with an eye on the future.

But I still didn't have enough to go solo.

The bank were still out.

BANK MANAGER: Good afternoon, Mr Turbo, how may I help you?

TERRY: You can start by giving me ten large to put a rave on, mate.

BANK MANAGER: Fuck it . . . here's twenty! Put two on!

It just doesn't happen, does it?

Hang about, though. What *do* banks give you money for?

I decided to get myself a house. Knowing someone who worked for the council, I had a word in his shell-like and an ex-council property was soon sorted out. That did two things: first, I rented it out, which brought in a steady income. That's something that bank managers like to see. Second, it got me in the door and sat in front of the geezer asking for a home improvement loan.

'Five thousand pounds to piss up the wall on a new bathroom suite and some roof tiles, Mr Turbo? Why, certainly.'

Now my little pot of cash was big enough to go for it.

The first official One Nation – fully under my control, with no interference – took place at Roller Express. If I say it myself, it was a ballsy move. I needed to make money from it, because I'd be fucked on the bank loan repayments otherwise. But that was a risk I had to take if I wanted to get anywhere. Understandably I was, let's say, apprehensive. In short, the night could make or break me. Thankfully, it went well, with around 2,000 people in: not full to busting, but good. I remember walking around the venue watching these people have a fucking great time, and knowing it was all down to me, and just feeling awesome.

Straight away, I'd got my mum involved. She sat in the cash box and she counted every penny in and every penny out. She'd done cashiering in a bookie's and had been an office manager, so she knew the score. Like I've said, if I didn't have a pair of eyes in there I may as well have dropped my pants at the door and bent over.

With mum watching the dough, the first rave made money – not a mountain, but some. So I was on course. Every new business needs time to establish itself, especially if it's a new club night because you have to build up a following. Luckily, I still had my bread and butter work coming in with the flying and *The Scene* to keep me alive and help me fund the raves.

The Island in Ilford was the venue for the next One Nation and this time we sold out. Another big, three thousand people capacity venue, another risk-taking, all-or-nothing, full-on event. I did it this way intentionally – I wasn't interested in starting small and taking forever to build it up. Maybe I was being a bit arrogant, but doing a rave for a few hundred people would have been the same as throwing a birthday party as far as I was concerned and didn't want to go back beyond square one. Jumping in at the deep end, knowing it was sink or swim, was the right kind of challenge – what would be the point of being safe? As the great philosopher Mr Derek Trotter once said: *He who dares, wins.*

I quickly worked out a formula. I tried to avoid anywhere where there'd been shootings or serious muggings, but – as you'll see later – that was next to fucking impossible. Three months out from a given event, I'd get my flyers designed: I drew it rough, always with a theme like 'Clash of the Titans', 'The Valentines Experience' or 'Payback', and my artist out in Kent, Damon from Design Asylum, would work them up from there. I called my company Diamond Promotions, so we'd have a little diamond on the front, and on the back would be a list of all our ticket outlets, phone lines – my mum manned them during the day, there were recorded messages at night – and everyone's mobile numbers. We'd have similar posters done for the record shops. DJs were starting to go through agents, so around this time I'd be sorting out my line-up with them – we were paying £100 to £150 a hour, something like that. My security team would be booked and sorted, and we'd have the tickets – watermarked and hologrammed – printed.

Six weeks out, we'd do a big mail out, and we'd also deliver flyers, posters and tickets to all the record shops, together with tapes of the previous event.

A week before, we'd advertise on Kiss FM and the best of the specialist drum'n'bass or garage pirate stations. Most of the DJs would be playing for us at some point or other, so they'd plug it and give away tickets.

In the early days, I'd have a meet on site with the production companies for the lights and sound, till they got to know what I wanted. They'd ask how much I wanted to spend. I'd do a ticket count and if the night was selling out I'd pay out a bit more. Most of the clubs had their own gear, so you were just topping them up – four or five grand would get you some lights, a laser and a smoke machine, and the normal bill would be anywhere between three and 10 large. Sometimes you'd beef up the sound, bring in some bass bins, other times you might have to build a stage for the DJs. We always took our own decks: you could guarantee the house ones would be fucked and the needle would go and they wouldn't have a spare and it would be a disaster. We'd always take our own mixer and monitor too.

Behind the scenes, I was always working. There was never time to relax, maybe five minutes here and there just for a breather, but never enough time for a break. It took around two hours to sort all the wages out, using a book with pre-written sales invoices in. If I asked any of the DJs or doormen for an invoice, they wouldn't know what the fuck I was on about, so I had to write them all out myself: From DJ Whoever to One Nation, here is an invoice for £X. I'd get them to sign it too.

Right from the off, I could see I was going to be making money. OK, not what I would if I'd started in the 1980s, when it was all *Accciiiid!*, yellow smiley faces and well underground. Back then, they found a field or broke into a warehouse, put some speakers and lights up, paid the DJs 50 quid each and 5,000 people turned up, each paying £25. None of this nonsense about insurance, or security. No costly advertising. Plus they were probably selling the kids the Es and whizz as well. At 3am, the party's in full swing, they just walk away with £150,000 cash in their back pockets. If it gets raided, who gives a fuck? The equipment's not theirs, so if it gets impounded they shrug their shoulders. Life's all about timing and, if I'd been around then, I'd have made millions and millions of pounds, and would now be living on my own island in the Pacific. That's if I hadn't been shot and buried in a shallow grave somewhere. Anyway, I wasn't around, so I'm not dead or a rave billionaire. Still, like I say, I was making serious money by my standards of the time. A good night could make me 10 grand. An average night, 5k. Usually it was somewhere in between.

The temptation to take cash rather than be legit was massive, of course. Early on, I yielded to that temptation, mainly because I thought it wouldn't last and that I ought to make hay while the sun shone. But as it got bigger and more professional, I realised I couldn't go on like that. The tax man and the VAT man were starting to spin DJs and other promoters and we were sure to get a knock. In the second year of business, I went to see an accountant.

It's the early to mid 90s, remember, and 500 quid a week was a lot of money. I was now making way more than that. I said, 'Listen, I haven't declared everything but I want to be clean. Can you sort it?'

So they went through all my stuff and then wrote off to the tax and VAT people without even telling me. Next thing I knew, I had the VAT man knocking on my door.

'Hello, Mr Turbo. You owe us 20 grand, or we're gonna come here and take all your stuff away.'

Once I'd picked myself up off the floor, I rang the accountant.

'What the fuck are you doing?' I said. 'I told you to sort my stuff out, not drop me in the shit and land me with a massive bill, you cunt.'

That was the end of that professional relationship. I switched accountants, going in with a lady called Frances Williams. She turned out to be a gem and an absolute Godsend. First, she arranged a payment schedule for me. Then she explained a few facts of life. And I needed them explaining: I'd never run a business before and I didn't have a family background in business or anything like that.

Frances said, 'Look, Terry, if you want to be legit you have to do it properly. You need to declare the money you make. You can take the odd small amount of petty cash but everything else has to go through the books.'

It was depressing advice, in a way, but it was sound advice, too. And I was glad I took it. I *liked* being clean. I could spend my dough without worrying that someone was looking over my shoulder all the time.

Early on, One Nation caused me problems with one or two of the promoters who used my Turbo Promotions for their flying. Because I was doing my own shows now, they thought I wasn't promoting theirs as full-on as I used to. Bollocks. I'd never do anything unless I gave it 100% – that's how I am. It was all jealousy but I had to smooth it over: my flyering wages were going straight back into One Nation, and I couldn't afford to lose the business.

My mum was a massive help. She ran the office and dealt with all the paperwork and chased up money, which left me free to do all the creative shit. I was always thinking of things that no one else had done – it was important for me to set myself apart from the others as much as I could, to be unique. I set a database up, from having names and addresses on the bottom of the tickets, where the punters could get free membership, a newsletter every few months and reductions on tickets and merchandise. We got some celeb lookalikes to attend our parties, which really made the night that bit special. We had the Queen one night: she did a meet and greet to people in the queue and walked around handing promo CDs out and even did a speech on stage. We had Prince William, Prince Charles, Madonna and Posh and Becks – they all just walked around, doing people's heads in. I bet there are people who still think to this day that they met David Beckham at a One Nation rave – and all their mates think they were on drugs. Well it *did* happen, you were right all along. My favourites were Ali G and Daniella Westbrook. The real ones. We got Sacha Baron Cohen just before he went massive – he was still perfecting Ali G and it was brilliant to get him there. Daniella appeared right after all that shit about her nose falling off. She went up on stage, took the mic and shouted, 'Just say no!' The crowd loved it.

We always had the best sound system I could afford, always the best lighting and laser display. I spared no expense because I knew what I wanted to see in a rave. I was a punter at heart, though I never went near the dance floor. I was too busy checking on security, sorting out DJs, making sure everything was running smoothly. I'd relax, a bit, around 3am. I might get up on the stage then and just look down at this sea of fucking people, all off their heads, going mental, loving it. In a way, I was jealous of them: I'd have loved to have been down there, going mad with them. But I also loved the fact that I'd created this myself.

We used to open the doors at nine at night and finish at six in the morning. I'd have around eight DJs in each room doing an hour each in a typical rave, with around four or five rooms. I had Drum 'n' Bass in the main room, Garage in the next room, Old Skool in the next, R 'n' B, and sometimes Stars of the Future, which gave all the up and coming DJs a chance, if we had another room.

Early on, I stuck to tried-and-tested venues like Roller Express, Club UN in Tottenham and the Island in Ilford. Rave venues were always, for some reason, in the shittest areas, places like Hackney, Dalston, Peckham, Romford. There was never one in fucking Hampstead.

We went from strength to strength, starting to build up a good name for ourselves with the punters and the clubs. The punters were obviously massively important, something that other promoters seemed to forget. Below the happy, smiling faces and the love-everyone vibe, there was always a lot of mugging and thieving on the rave scene: not everyone was on-one-matey, there for the unity and the music. I always remembered my own experiences as a young raver. One winter night particularly stuck in my mind – a party at the Labyrinth club in Dalston, Hackney. I drove all the way from Camberley with a bunch of mates and we parked a kick up the arse away from the club. Even on the way to the club from the car, we thought we were going to get mugged: it was crawling with shifty-looking geezers hiding in shadows and following us to the doors. I was paranoid about coming back out of the place if that's how bad it was getting *in* the fucker, but we still had a really good night. When we got to the car a good seven hours later, all the windows had been smashed in. It was freezing cold, we were sweating from the club and we were practically frozen solid by the time we got home. I had the heater on the dashboard blasting onto my face but didn't feel any of it. From then on, I fucking hated that place and I never went back. I wasn't going to have my own punters turning against my venues and events like that. We worked fucking hard to keep the scum out and a lot of ravers came to our clubs because they knew they'd be safe. No one worked harder, anywhere in the country, because no one else cared as much about their customers. I remember doing flyers once outside a competitor's rave. I was talking to the promoter when a geezer came walking up. 'Are you in charge?' he asked.

The promoter barely acknowledged him, looked at him like he thought the kid was nothing.

'I've just been mugged,' he said.

'So what do you want me to do about it?' asked the promoter.

Bang out of order. For starters, men don't like admitting to being mugged and it must have taken a lot of courage for this guy to do that. To make matters worse, he'd now been made to look a right cunt by the promoter. I wanted to give the promoter a clump, but I was there asking him for money I was owed. He really didn't care about anything other than his bank balance and his attitude was shit. I know you can't sort out everything, but you can at least try.

Our approach worked for the clubs, too. There were a lot of dodgy, fly-by-night promoters on the scene so I struck deals where we'd hire a place for the rest of the year, provided they didn't let promoter X and promoter Y have it during that time. I'd pay them a grand's deposit up front, and it was a win-win: they could plan ahead and I could make sure the venue didn't earn a reputation as Mugger Central because it wasn't being hired out to any shit promoters. Half of the time, the venue saw the benefits and said yes, because good promoters were hard to find. They knew I was in it as a career and that I gave a shit about the venue, the staff, the music, the atmosphere, the bar and the punters. I wasn't just there to run a thousand raves in a year and fuck off into the sunset laughing. If I hired, they were guaranteed to get paid on time every time, that I'd pack the place to capacity and that there wouldn't be any aggro. It was a club owner's dream.

Of course, a lot of them didn't see it like that. Typically, they charged £10,000 to hire a place. That's a lot of money to fork out just for a night and once they started counting the tenners their eyes lit up. They started trying to hire the venue out every night, to any fucker, and if they added a few greedy extras on top they could make a hundred grand in a week, easily. So what if the promoter was shit, and the rave attracted scum? They didn't give a flying fuck. If there were any incidents, it was nothing to do with the venue: as long as the building was still standing the next day, it was a success. Totally irresponsible. I'm all for packing a place out to get the best out of a crowd and a venue, but not mixing a bunch of decent punters with any amount of scumbags. The knock-on effect was that the police began shutting some events down because they weren't safe to go to. We never had that problem.

Our crowds got bigger and better and the buzz around One Nation started getting really serious. By now, I was making good money out of every event I did – a really good night would clear me 20 large.

We boosted the income with tape packs. At each event, we'd have a line into the decks recording the DJs and the sounds: afterwards, we'd take the raw tape to a production house and they'd stick it onto C60 tapes. Eight of them would cover the whole night, and we could knock them out at 20 quid a pop. You might sell 500 or even 1,000 of them, which was nice additional bunce. We sold them through the record shops, who also flogged our tickets, and the kids would call in every week or two, pick up a new One Nation tape pack and then drive round in their XR3i with it blasting out of the sunroof annoying everyone. The tapes went everywhere, and sold in their thousands. I remember the police questioned me once about where we sold them. Some bird had been raped in a house and there'd been a One Nation tape playing in the background. I had to tell them it could have been any one of several hundred shops. Not the best advert for One Nation, but not much we could do about it.

It wasn't all plain sailing – nothing is. I ran a rave at the Adrenaline Village, squeezed an extra night into my schedule because I was getting greedy. It sounded simple: every time I put an event on, I'm walking away with a minimum of 10 grand in my pocket. So why not just do more events? I learned a painful lesson about greed. I picked the wrong night, it was a disaster and I lost £10,000 instead of making it. That is a lot of money to lose and I was fucking devastated. Apart from anything else, it wasn't like I could afford to lose it. Although I was earning a lot, I was spending a lot, too – some was going back into One Nation and some was going on clothes, cars and birds. The rest was being saved for the rainy day I always anticipated and I didn't want to dip into that unless I absolutely had to. A lot of promoters weren't like that. They'd do an event, make 20 grand and go on holiday for a month. They'd do a load of gear, fuck a load of hookers, go shopping and come back potless, thinking, *Right, better do another event.* They had no plans for the future. I wasn't like that. For every pound I spent, I tried to put a pound away. I'm a worrier: when you start off in life with nothing, and then you get something, you're always scared you're going to lose it all and you'll end up back on the council estate with no money. It's always hanging over you and driving you on, and to me it's a healthy fear to have.

This had been the first serious knock I'd taken and I could see the Old Dean looming: I teetered on the edge of jacking it all in and going back to get a proper job somewhere. Assuming I could find one. I didn't want to chuck good money after bad.

But I had a stern word with myself, dusted myself down, and carried on, vowing not to do anything as silly again. The chances were I would, but I'd deal with that if and when it happened.

Wembley was my way of trying to pull things back. It was probably the best party One Nation ever put on – May 1996 at Wembley Arena. Ravers still talk about it now: we teamed up with Fusion (Hardcore) and Gism (House and Garage) to put on the biggest do ever seen at that point. We called it *A Match Made At*

Wembley. There were 10,000 punters there and it was fucking phenomenal. It was nutty, too. We had break dancing fairies playing bongos, the stage was done up like an American street – all graffitied up and with old road signs – and the crowning glory was when we blew a police car up on the stage. I wish to fuck I'd been there as a dancer because it must have been a legendary experience for the clubbers. For the promoters, it was a fucking headache, despite all the fun. We had loads of aggro; even with 30 of our own doormen on, it was non-stop from beginning to end. They really earned their wages. We had people rushing the door, a guy was stabbed, a girl claimed she'd been raped (a doctor later confirmed she hadn't been touched), and there were muggings and fighting all through the night. We had to deal with it all. At one point, we linked arms and swept through the venue in riot police formation to hunt out anyone causing aggro. If we found anyone, we broke the line momentarily and one of the lads would punch his head in – with our usual hit first, hit hard and hit fast policy, making the first punch count so there was no chance of a fight.

Concerned punters kept asking if we caught the rapist all night and it was doing my fucking head in. It was such a pig of a night that my mum told me she was going off working for me. I was fucked when we finished and I only managed to make six grand out of it, which wasn't really worth getting out of bed for. I know that sounds ridiculous, but I was expecting to make 10 times that. So that really fucked me off money-wise, too.

I'd obviously calmed my own lifestyle down a lot at this point. Drugs, birds and raving go hand in hand. There's no getting away from it.

As a punter going out and clubbing all the time, I had no problem with being surrounded by drugs and seeing all these people off their heads.

As a promoter, obviously things are different. When you're at work, it's a total no-no. This was a serious business and I was in it to make money. You can't function if you're out of your head on class As all the time. Too many have tried and failed. In fact, if you ask me, if you have *anything* stronger than a fucking Red Bull, you might as well throw the towel in immediately. You saw what happened to Paul and Ralph – and I don't just mean drugs make you wear comedy hats and write shit magazines.

Apart from that, the Old Bill could close you down if they found your venues awash with pills. So you had to make a strong show of keeping them out. We would batter the fuck out of dealers who got out of line and search people coming in – even full body cavity searches, eventually – but still some of it would get through, just the same as with the smugglers bringing stuff into the UK in the first place, or into jail, for fuck's sake.

If I ever got asked, I'd point to the searches and stuff but the truth was that, while we didn't want dealers or punters taking the piss, drugs were an essential part of the rave scene so we did our bit and then stood back and let them get on with it. Dancing was what drugs were designed for, and what better place to get off your tits and have fun for ten hours than with a few thousand other likeminded ravers, some banging tunes and a mind-blowing light show? Most people in most raves were off their head on something. It was how the scene worked. As long as they were 18 or over, it was really between them, the law and the NHS, at the end of the day.

In the early days of the Acid House thing, it was a bit of puff, speed to stay up longer, sometimes mixed with acid. The E came along and after that it was open season – GHB, ketamine, coke and all the dirty stuff like crack and heroin.

I'm not scared to admit that I had dabbled in my early days of raving. But having seen addiction first hand, in my dad's alcoholism, and being around so many people off their faces on drugs, I was never going to go the same way. People changed – their behaviour, their attitude and personalities altered, some-times for the better, in the short term – ecstasy single-handedly put a stop to football hooliganism – but generally for the worse over time. One geezer I knew had got his bird a wrap of speed and got himself a wrap of coke. He gave her the coke by mistake and she went to the toilets to bomb the wrap. While she was gone he discovered he'd given her the wrong wrap. He went mad with her for necking it when it was his own stupid fault.

I've also seen what crack does to people – I've seen them on their hands and knees picking little bits of fluff and toe nails and things off their own living room floor in case it was something else they could get high on. It was fucking disgusting, degenerate behaviour and it made my skin scrawl. Examples like that should be used as Just Say No adverts.

I don't know many people who have been part of the rave scene without experimenting with drugs, and those who say they haven't are probably lying. Even Bill Clinton admitted to trying a bit of puff a few years back (although he didn't inhale, did he?). Come to think of it, he did not have sexual relations with that woman either. What a fucking geezer – he'd be great to go out on the piss with.

'I did not smash that man's head in.'

OK, Bill, be on your way now, you scallywag.

Accepting drugs was something you had to do in a new culture. When I was going to all the Sharon and Tracey bars, it was accepted that everyone would binge-drink as much as possible, try to fuck some slapper, probably have a fight and get a kebab on the way home. At a rave, drinking so much alcohol dehydrates you and sends you to sleep when you want to dance your arse off all night. Drugs make most people feel great, they dance, they drink water and they enjoy the night as much as the geezer in the kebab shop at kicking out time.

I'd said goodbye to my excesses in 1994, knowing it was time to knuckle down and start being the kind of person I'd been striving to become. It was the best thing I ever did – I love having a few drinks every now and then these days, because there's nothing better than relaxing on a night out. Back then, I didn't even drink very often. I was running raves all the time, doing flyers, writing a magazine, phoning people, picking stuff up, designing flyers, meeting people, arranging everything and trying to pick women up at the same time – I didn't have recreational time for recreational drugs.

GETTING A TEAM TOGETHER

L ike I said, most raves were in shitty areas and there were muggers and scum everywhere. Plus, the industry itself wasn't exactly a boardroom-and-golf-club kind of thing. The fuck-up at the Rocket with Phil and Mick had been a good pointer there. Organising and promoting raves had no regulations and procedures in place. It was full of people who were earning money on their own terms and usually by strong-arm tactics. Financial predictions and five-year-plans were unheard of – people would get someone to back them, and they'd drop £10,000 off in used 20s the next day. These were tough-talking, hard bastards who were used to operating outside of the law. It was an arena where the big boys played – if you couldn't hold your own, you were in the wrong business. That was how it worked.

I was handy enough but I was in my early 20s, a bit out my depth, one man standing up to geezers in their 30s. Right from the start, before the first solo Roller Express do, I'd realised I needed a team around me – a team of the hardest, meanest, nastiest bastards London had to offer. If I had them behind me, then I had power and everyone would be a lot more wary of me. Additionally, we could keep all those nasty wankers out of the venues and our punters safe. Each venue would have its own lot looking after the door, but they were mostly a waste of space and they wouldn't have my interests at heart.

It wasn't as easy as it sounds. I needed loyal guys, who were reliable and very fucking hard, and they don't come easy or cheap. Every firm has a one or two of them, but it also has its fair share of shitbags and wannabes. Places like Roller Express, once I got established there, and the local criminals knew I was making money, would be like magnets. I knew I'd have every low-life, knife-carrying mugging cunt trying to get in and rob my clubbers and I needed to be able to stamp on them with maximum ferocity.

I hit on a unique idea. From being around for a few years, clubbing and getting into a few scrapes, I knew a few tasty geezers – the head doormen at places like Laserdrome, Labyrinth, the main guy at Roller Express itself, lots like that. What if I just went to the head boys and asked them – no-one else on their team, just them – to work for me for one night, every now and then? If I doubled their wages, the chances were they'd go for it. By doing one event a month for me, they'd make double pay and be able to take a night off from their other job if they wanted.

Every geezer I went to was a proper hardcore wrecking machine who would have it with anyone and not back down. I needed lads who were prepared to deal with anything that came their way and would fight to the death if need be.

Everyone I approached signed up.

People couldn't believe it. No one had ever seen a group like this in the same room together and now I had them on the same firm and under my supervision. All it took was having the balls to ask.

I knew I was onto a winner. They were the best there was and I had a dozen or so of them. Ten of the best can stand up to a tasty crew of 30, easily. I needed my lot to control venue staff anywhere we went so they wouldn't take any liberties.

I didn't just want hard nuts, though. I also needed them to be polite and friendly to the average Joe punter. I didn't want a firm who would just stand around intimidating people, because they'd just go somewhere else next time. I worked out that doormen could be a selling point: a rave had to be an *experience* from the moment you turned up at the front door, and a chatty, smiling door team helps that start. People feel wanted. Of course, most doormen are pretty friendly these days. Back then, in the 1990s, before licensing and PLCs running everything, we were almost unique. There was no thought of customer service on 99.9% of doors. Instead, you had knuckle-dragging idiots, guys who'd claim they'd killed people, the ones who were dealers on the sly or who let people serve up, the ones who were itching for a fight if you said Hello, and the ones who don't let you in because they had a row with the missus on their way to work.

My firm – the Hit Squad – became legendary on the rave scene. We worked together, became friends, and then became family.

So let's meet a few of the boys.

Warrior from South London was my first choice. He's a big, black, scary geezer – still working now, even into his forties. He worked at the Roller Express as their clean-up man; if anyone stepped out of line he'd deal with them on the spot. People were petrified of him because he was a Warrior. He used to carry a samurai sword down his back under his shirt, and was known to have various other instruments of pain in his possession. Not that he needed them; it was just his way of being even scarier. He didn't give a fuck and would use extreme violence without any hesitation if he had to. I'd say Warrior was more of a deterrent than anything else. You just had to take one look at him and you knew not to give him any grief. When I introduced him to people, he could scare them to death if he was in that kind of mood. No one would make eye contact with him unless they had to. His conversations were beyond mad; he'd do and say bizarre things that made perfect sense to him and would make me laugh, but to any outsiders he was a very dangerous man.

Next, Gary Gooner. I met Gary Gooner in Stonebridge. He used to run the doors at a moody sports centre there that put on reggae nights. He's an enigma: a very articulate, well-spoken guy with impeccable manners, in a way that completely throws you off guard. He's this huge six-foot-six black geezer, and when you know he's a doorman, you expect him to throw his weight around and conform to type. Gary's not like that. He's a really nice bloke . . . until you cross him.

He was a time-served Arsenal football hooligan and totally streetwise, having worked the West Indian circuit. When I came calling, he was in a bit of trouble and was looking for some work. What a geezer he turned out to be – he was a natural, knowing exactly what to look for in a club and how to respond to it, knowing all and seeing all like a Jedi master. I remember one time when Gary hadn't even had chance to get inside the venue before I called on him for backup.

He was walking towards us when I spotted him. 'Gary,' I shouted. 'Those cunts have just robbed these girls.'

A couple of birds had just had their tickets swiped and the geezers were making off down the road with them.

Gary played it very cool. 'What?' he shouted back. 'Those two boys there? I think there's been a mistake.' He called out to them, 'Excuse me, chaps. Could you just come back here, please?'

They came back. Gary sounded so nice and polite people often imagined he was a soft touch. 'Do you mind telling me where you got your tickets from?' he asked them.

'Them two girls over there with your mate just gave them to us,' said one of the lads.

Gary acted like he believed them, and sweet-talked them into coming my way for the girls to identify them. When they were confirmed as the robbers, Gary knocked them clean out on the spot. None of us even saw how he did it. I knew he'd moved, I saw that much, but I'd never seen anyone get knocked out so quickly. It was like he something out of a Chuck Norris movie . . . only it was real. So I took it as my cue to follow in and start booting them to fuck.

Adam Saint was more of a friend who helped me out and looked after me out of loyalty rather than anything else. He deserves a mention as part of the firm because of everything he did for me and the boys. Known as The Sheriff in his area – he was the geezer who sorted out all the trouble and knew everything that went on. No-one messed with him; they went to him for protection, help, everything. Another hulk of a geezer with hands like shovels, he's as polite and friendly as Gary and has amazing presence. He can walk into any room anywhere and own it. All through self-confidence and how he conducts himself.

We had mutual friends – Chris Brown from United Dance, Slipmatt – but never knew each other till we met at one of Chris's events one night and clicked. We're like a pair of brothers in some ways – Wilf Pine once said he'd never seen two blokes handle themselves like us since Ron and Reg Kray. Some people may not take that as a compliment – I did, because I'd never had confidence as a kid and for someone like Wilf to notice it meant a lot. Adam was refreshing, self-made and one of the best friends a bloke could ask for.

Boogie is a small black guy who you could really come unstuck with. He wasn't your stereotypical doorman – he wasn't very tall or heavily built. People would try to take advantage of him because of his size, assuming he couldn't handle himself. Big mistake. He is heavy-duty, as anyone who tried it on soon found out. Boogie had a very quick temper and could go off at any time. He became my head guy and was with me from day one until the day I sold the business. It was his job to collect all my money in from the raves and debts . . . and we *always* got paid. I think that says everything.

One night, at the Island in Ilford, I was standing having a conversation with someone. It must have been a blue moon if I was stood in one place for longer than 10 seconds. As I was talking, this geezer came flying down the stairs unconscious. Nothing out of the ordinary there, except that his cock was hanging out. *What the fuck's going on?* Then Boogie came running down the stairs, calling him a dirty bastard and carried on punching and kicking him, before dragging him outside.

A couple of minutes later, he came back in, sweating and angry. I didn't want to think about the poor twat he'd just left outside. 'What was that all about?' I said.

'Dirty bastard was pissing all up the stairs,' said Boogie. 'I had to teach him some fucking manners.'

That's Boogie. He never took any shit. Or piss, for that matter.

Billie was and still is an absolute madman. He was probably one of the most dangerous blokes we had because, like Boogie, he was small and not what you'd expect a doorman to look like. When the two of them were partnered up they were unstoppable. With some distance between you, you'd think you could take him. Up close, mouthing off at him, you'd suddenly realise you'd made a big fucking mistake. By then, it would be too late because he was quicker than greased lightning. I'd never laid eyes on him until I went down to World Dance to recruit him, having heard all about this bloke's fearsome reputation. I asked around and this little fella wandered over.

'Hi, I'm Billie,' he said.

'*You're* not Billie,' I replied.

'Alright, I'm not Billie, mate,' and he turned round to walk off. I was used to people pulling stunts like that. Of course it wasn't fucking *Billie*. To be a top geezer on the doors, you had to be over six foot tall and built like a tank, unless you were Boogie. As it happened, Boogie was standing next to me. 'That fucking *is* Billie, you twat,' he said.

I called him back. 'Hi Billie, I'm Terry. Sorry about the misunderstanding.'

Luckily, he saw the funny side.

He was Boogie's top doorman. We ran a Garage Nation event in Options one New Year's Eve and it all kicked off in a big way. A gang of Asian geezers came in started upsetting couples, getting in between them and touching the women up. Because there were so many of them, no one was fronting up to them and they were just taking the piss out of anyone they wanted. Until the firm stepped in. Billie and Boogie went over to see what was going on and saw a mate of ours get a slap from one of the gang.

Billie pushed his way in straight away. 'Look guys,' he said.

'It's New Year. We want a peaceful night, so let's just keep it that way, OK?'

'What you gonna do about it?' was the geezer's somewhat stereotypical reply.

Why? Why the fuck can't these people just behave, just let it go? Someone's going to get badly hurt, and it might end up being them. It's fucking beyond me.

This lad squared up to Billie and kept asking him what he was going to do.

Eventually, Billie answered him.

It wasn't with a punch. Instead, he hit him with the palm of his hand, right beneath the chin. The impact lifted the boy a few feet and left him sparked clean out in a pile of spilled drinks and smashed glasses. Of course, a few of his mates steamed in. I dunno . . . perhaps they hadn't been paying attention. Despite the numbers against them, Billie and Boogie didn't bother looking for back-up. They just dived in and started smashing anyone up who got in their way, scattering people everywhere and sending tables and chairs flying. Billie got a bottle of champagne smashed over his head – have you ever felt the weight of a champagne bottle, the thickness of the glass? – but it just spurred him on further. The two of them cleared out this entire gang of Asian fuckwits in the space of a few minutes.

I wasn't there, but I heard all about it a bit later.

'What happened?' I said.

'Some cunt smashed a bottle of champagne over my head.'

'Fucking hell . . . are you ok?'

'Yeah, I'm fine, But the guy who hit me isn't,' he chuckled.

The boys were all pissing themselves. You could smash anything off Billie's head and he'd just turn round and kick your fucking teeth in.

Jon Jon is an absolute man-mountain, like The Thing from *Fantastic Four*, and a legend on the south coast. He's in his early 50s now – two daughters, three granddaughters and his girlfriend is the same age as one of his daughters. He got the name because of his size – he's like two people, like a fucking wall, and has been in the security business all his life, running his own company for 20 years and employing nearly 400 doormen. In the early 90s he used to run a few clubs, so for an 'old man' he was well clued up on his rave music. He was a mate of Wilf Pine's and as my friendship with Wilf grew, he suggested Jon Jon could come up to help me out on raves. Another known for his sense of humour, Jon Jon was utterly deadpan. One time at the Rex, he was stood at the back doors stopping all the little fuckers trying to sneak in. It was a freezing cold night and he was wearing a balaclava. The geezers who owned the Rex were reputed to be a heavy-duty Irish firm connected to the IRA in some way – it was probably bollocks, but that was the story. The area manager came to visit and told me that Jon Jon wearing a balaclava was a bit sensitive. All he needed was an Armalite and a republican flag. 'We don't want anyone thinking we are trying to wind people up,' he said.

'Maybe so,' I said 'You go and tell him.' He could wear a Mickey Mouse mask for all I cared, as long as he did a good job. The bloke went to tell Jon Jon to take the balaclava off and was told to go fuck himself. Jon was a man of very few words but he was always charming.

Mr Magoo was like a walking 32-stone pharmacy. No one knows if he was named after the cartoon character, he just came with the name. Drugs-wise, he'd done everything imaginable and most substances we confiscated didn't even make it to the drug box without him having a dab or two. We took a bag of powder once, which we assumed was Charlie. Magoo necked the lot of it and passed out in the cash box. The bird who was working in there at the time just used him as a seat.

He loved life, and had no qualms about eating the right food or any of that bollocks – he just did what he wanted. He had narcolepsy: he'd fall asleep any time, any place, any where . . . we should have called him Martini, not Magoo. He was given some stuff by the doctor, some tablets that were basically amphetamines to keep him awake, but he took his entire month's dosage in one go and stayed up for a week, then kept falling asleep for the following three. Once he nodded off at my gaff, so I got on top of him and started surfing with my arms stretched out and the rest of the lads singing the theme to *Hawaii Five-O*.

He woke up and said, 'What the fuck are you doing on my back?'

'Surfing,' I said.

Then he went back to sleep.

He's done it everywhere. He dozed off while he was under his car fixing it once – the neighbours thought he was dead and called the police and ambulance and they were just about to call the fire brigade in to winch him out when he woke up and started shouting, 'What the fuck do you lot want? Get off my property.'

He fell asleep while getting something out the oven – we were going to put his head in, for a laugh, but decided not to – he flattened at least two coffee tables, he nodded off on the bog (we brushed his teeth with the toilet brush) and then fell off it so we couldn't open the door to wake him. Jon Jon's dog used to stay well out of his shadow, if that was possible.

Having said all that, he was a hard, hard man. He would go through crowds like a rhino, always the last man standing and respected by everyone. The sight of him and Jon Jon coming for you would be enough to make you shit your pants. Make no mistake; you'd have to keep running forever to escape them. Even if Magoo couldn't be bothered to punch your face in, he could just sleep on you and you'd be fucked.

His pancreas gave out in the end. When he knew his innings was coming to a close, he went and bought a fuck-off speed boat. He didn't give a fuck.

Jez B was known as The Bad Boy. He was hard as nails for a relatively young geezer, and a champion cage fighter – I think he has around seven titles. I met Jezza at the Caribbean Club in Basingstoke when we were both 'up-and-coming' MCs, which translates to shit MCs. It was a place where you could do something like that and get away with it because there was such an amazing atmosphere. He must have been around 16 years old and I was around 19 and we got to know each other through friends of friends. We became closer in around 2000, after losing touch through various reasons, mainly to do with me spending every working minute on promoting. Jez had his own interests and we drifted apart as you sometimes do. But then we met up again somewhere and clicked, just like old times. I asked him if he fancied doing a bit of work for me.

He came to work for me at One Nation because we always had such a laugh together – it was even better when he was training for a fight and working for me because he was an angry cunt. Even when we got into fights, I couldn't help find something funny in it. Some shit kicked off with a couple of geezers at a club because I'd bumped into one of them while dragging some other idiot out. He puffed his chest out and came at me, so I cracked him spark out. Another came forward and Jez let fly with a one-two and floored this other geezer. It was all for no reason! Why did they have to do it? I couldn't help laughing at the way it happened.

'Come on, you cun-' BANG!

'Right, you cun-' BANG-BANG!!

That was two of them knocked out in two seconds flat. I lent over the one I'd decked, and in my most American accent, said, 'You got knocked the fuck out!' and 'Someone better call a doctor!', adding a little dance to it.

I've been to Vegas a few times with Jez in recent years and we've always got into some scrapes. There are some friends of ours out there who Wilf knows and they always look after us when we are in town. They call me The Crazy Englishman. I always goad Jez into a fight with someone, then I hide when he turns round for back-up – all he can hear is me laughing away somewhere like a lunatic. The last time we were over there, a geezer spilt some champagne down Jez's back in a club. It was no big deal but something about the geezer – I think it was that he was such an arrogant prick – meant I felt it was my duty to do something about it.

So I wound Jez up with things like, 'Who does that fucker think he is?' and 'Look. Him and his mates are looking over and laughing at you. What the fuck are you going to do about it? You gonna let this prick mug you off like that?'

I said I'd be right behind him – let's go and sort the lot of them out. Jez was psyched up and steamed over to them, demanding apologies and telling them that we'd give them a kicking. When he turned for me to join in, I was sat across the other side of the room pissing myself.

He banned me from going to watch him fight because he can always hear me laughing if he gets beat. The last time was a fight in Bracknell with some American geezer who'd fought in the UFC. The ref stopped the fight in the American guy's favour. Jez told me that when the ref announced his loss to the crowd, all he could hear was me laughing. I fucking love it.

Don't get me wrong – he's one of the soundest, solidest guys you'll ever meet – I'd trust him to the ends of the earth and I love him like a brother . . . as I do all the guys who stood with me all those years.

Matt and The Animal were both spawned in Gravesend and they were both really dangerous boys. Matt's a great mate and an absolute legend. The Animal . . . well, you don't get called Animal for being good at cake decorating, do you? At about six-foot-four and 18 stone, he used to run the doors in Plymouth and would beat Royal Marines two or three at a time just for a laugh. And that was on his nights off. He was unhinged at the best of times and wouldn't stop in a fight until you were completely fucked – he'd open you up and leave you lying there on the floor. He only worked for us on the odd occasion with Matt – who was in *Hell to Pay*, incidentally, in the pub scene where I wind Jeremy Bailey up.

The Sanctuary in Milton Keynes springs to mind when I remember Animal. We were standing in a fenced off compound having a coffee, when a bunch of good-for-nothing hood-rats thought it would be a good idea to rush the door, trying to get in for free. Animal had them in his sights. As soon as they started running towards the fence he ran at the other side of it, picked it up, and smashed straight into them, possessed, growling. He overpowered them immediately – it was no contest really, they were floored by his power and ended up on the floor with not only a fucking huge metal fence on top of them, but also with Animal jumping up and down all over it, squashing the breath out of them, screaming and shouting and foaming at the mouth like, well . . . like an animal. It was scary to watch but highly amusing at the same time. We were there to sort the bad guys out, after all. He just happened to sort five of them out in one go – creative, as well as dangerous. Of all the doormen I knew, I'd say he was the scariest because no one could stop him or control him.

Mark aka R.S. was a guy I met at Adrenaline Village. He used to sell tools – and not Black & Decker ones. Whatever you wanted, he had it: knuckledusters, gas, coshes, bats, knives, you name it. I think my favourites were leather gloves with pieces of metal sewn into the knuckles. He used to turn up in his Range Rover and open the back up to pedal his wares to the kind of people who used street weapons as part of their job. Basically it was like a mobile sweetshop for doormen and he'd give his card out if you needed anything urgently.

I'd been having some hassles with one or two people and it looked like it might get a bit naughty. Someone gave me Mark's number so I gave him a bell. I explained who I was and he agreed to meet up with me out in the sticks, because he didn't allow home visits. It was like some fucking spy film, all secrets and exact times and I thought he was a right weirdo. When he turned up, he started scanning me with some device saying he was checking me out. I said I only wanted to buy a few tools off him, not propose marriage. He was a bit eccentric to say the least, but I must have passed his test because we ended up round at his gaff.

'How far do you want to go?' he asked.

His missus was well pissed off. 'I'll tell you how far I'm going,' she said. 'I'm off to fucking bed.'

And then I realised that he'd had a few sherbets.

He showed me his collection of arms . . . he had French military distress flares, grenades, devices for grabbing people's wrists with and breaking them, special coshes, torture equipment, night vision goggles . . . the works. He was ex-Parachute Regiment, had done some mercenary stuff and close protection and I thought he'd be perfect to get in the firm. I used to call him Inspector Gadget because of all the stuff he had on him – he was like a cross between that and Q in James Bond, with gizmos for every occasion. I have no idea where he got this stuff, who made it or *how* they made it . . . one night he brought a machine for scanning people carrying drugs. We used to call it The Wand. He'd wave this thing at people and say, 'Empty your pockets,' and you could guarantee they'd be carrying. Fuck knows how it worked. It just did. It was legendary to the point that people would see it and go walking up the street to get rid of their gear, which was funny.

Nick was an ex-Special Forces dog handler who brought in our One Nation resident Psycho Dog, Bruscoe. Nick was scary enough, but Bruscoe was the real deal. He was without a doubt the scariest Doberman/doorman of them all. He was trained in German commands, and could rip bollocks off or tear throats apart if needed. You couldn't even say hello to Nick because as soon as you got within biting distance, Bruscoe would fucking have you. He gave us the kind of back-up no man can and the pair of them made an awesome team, working almost telepathically. When he wasn't working, he loved to play in the garden and do all normal doggy things. But as soon as he heard his German commands, you didn't stand a chance. He was a brilliant doordog – I'd much rather have someone try to sue me for a dog ripping his hand off than have to deal with someone being shot dead at my club. That was the reality of it.

Scooby. He wasn't another psycho dog; he got the name

because he was a real joker and great fun to have around. Scooby was a 30-something half caste bodybuilder from Milton Keynes. He was funny but he could have a row with anyone. He used to run the doors at Jongleurs Comedy Club in Camden. I organised a Christmas party there one year for around 20 of us and we must have looked like we were on night release from Pentonville clink, all with shaved heads, all six-footers, all likely to react badly to having the piss taken by a comedian in a comedy club. Scooby was bricking it, telling us not to get lairy and saying he wouldn't mind if we went elsewhere. Yeah, right.

The comedian couldn't resist a few snide comments about us and Warrior took offence. You always hear how a lot of comedians started in the playground at school when they used to shame all the bullies with their wit and win people over. We weren't in the playground now, though, and the comedian was the one starting it. If there's a bunch of really hard-looking geezers, is it worth taking the piss to see if they'll laugh? Just concentrate on someone else. Warrior fought back and started heckling the comedian; Pussyhole, Bumpaclaat, and Federali were some of the words he shouted at him. He was on quite a roll – even the other punters in there laughed at his heckling, and it wasn't just nervous laughter, he was genuinely funny.

However, Warrior had smoked enough gear and drank enough brandy to give Dr fucking Dre a whitey. He was convinced that the comedian was working for the government and decided that he had to kill him after the show. Fucking hell – the guy was only joking! For safety reasons, he was bundled into a cab after his routine and Warrior eventually calmed down. He (and his Samurai sword) would deal with the geezer another day. Just because it was Christmas, didn't mean he had to carve someone up.

Big Albert was a big, black bodybuilder and it was through him that I met Scooby and Gary Gooner. He was fucking huge, this geezer. A house-husband that looked after his two kids better than any woman I know would have done, he was a real nice guy with an equally dark side. Albert was one of those who I could trust implicitly and rely on in any situation. Albert was with me at The Island in Ilford when we caught a mugger using a knife and picking on smaller, weaker geezers.

We dragged him upstairs. Instead of just punching into him, we let him have a chance.

'No weapons. Let's see what you've got,' I said.

Albert stood and told the geezer to take the first punch. The geezer turned into a little boy before our eyes.

'No,' he said.

'I thought you was a tough guy?' said Albert. 'Come on. You can sort other people out, try and sort me out. Take a swing. Go on.'

The guy started to cry. Sobbing like a baby. His knife was on the desk and we put something next to it for him to compare the two and to show him we meant business. I made him take his clothes off and I smacked him about to emphasise my point. Then we fucked him off out of there.

Ken and Jim were a fucking mental double act who I used to box with. Ken's white and six-foot-four, Jim's black and six-foot-one. They were ex-Parachute Regiment and were great friends as well as very disciplined, no-nonsense guys. Jim and I were in the gym sparring one day, he was orthodox and I'm a southpaw. I kept standing on his foot and giving him a right hook in the chops – an old boxers trick my granddad taught me – and he lost the plot big style. He really fucking went for me and we ended up rolling around the floor beating the shit out of each other like some UFC piss-take. The club's trainer went mad and told us if we ever went off on one and lost control again, he would throw us out of the club. I called it improvising, not losing control. He should watch more Tyson fights. I lost touch with Ken, but I know Jim is working as a mercenary in Iraq at the moment.

Eddie Stokes was a serious man. Repeat – serious. Another one with a military background, he was feared by everyone who knew him. Get in his way and you got knocked to fuck. No messing. He was a martial arts expert and enjoyed hurting people. I went on a martial arts week with him in Gran Canaria called The Gathering of the Masters. I was a Purple belt in Ju-Jitsu at the time. Every night Eddie wanted to go and have a fight in a bar with some random punter and practice the martial arts moves he'd learned that day on anyone who wanted it. Or didn't want it. He was a scary fucker indeed. I'm all for learning techniques and how to fight, but I didn't see the point in taking that kind of knowledge to someone on the street. On the way over, I said I was looking forward to training with him and he laughed and said, 'No Terry. I'm gonna really hurt some of these cunts.' He kept his word.

One night we were on our way back from a One Nation event at Bagleys in Kings Cross and Eddie was moaning on about having stomach ache. He confessed to having a burger from the dreaded Bagleys burger van that you would never go to, even if you were starving to death.

'Ha ha! You've probably got food poisoning or mad cow disease.' I chuckled. The lads were pissing themselves. 'No Eddie. Please tell me you didn't really eat one of those burgers from the van.' The situation deteriorated, until Eddie shouted, 'Turbo . . . pull the fuck over!'

As politely requested, I pulled the fuck over and we spent 10 minutes watching him chuck his guts up at the side of the road. What's so funny about watching your friend being violently ill at seven am on a Sunday morning at the side of a motorway? I'm fucked if I know. It was just really funny.

When he finished and we set off, we were all still chuckling like school kids, 'You fucking cunts. I hope you all die.' he said.

And he probably meant it too. He could charm anyone, Eddie.

Terry Fisher was another great guy. Very hard, a real team player who would never take a step back. He's a funny guy, too: one of the few people who can have a pistol pulled on him by a 17-year-old crackhead over a stolen ticket he's just confiscated... and laugh about it.

Carlton Leach was a good mate and our Essex Connection if things got tasty out that way. Carlton's a very tough man with a reputation for loyalty to his friends and not someone you'd want to cross. Having him as a friend and ally was always a bonus, and that friendship has led to us writing and making a film about his life; called *Rise Of The Footsoldier*, it will be released in UK cinemas in the Autumn of 2007. (Check out www.riseofthefoot soldier.com)

Pikki and Temper were a couple of real south Londoners that you wouldn't want to cross. Ever. They never actually worked for me, we were just really good friends. They always came to One Nation and we always got the red carpet and VIP treatment ready for them. They looked out for me, and we've remained mates ever since. (Pikki recently produced *Rollin' with the Nines* where I played a corrupt cop – more of that later.)

Pinto and Tuffy . . . now, these two were not only hilarious but they should have been called double the danger. I have never seen anyone go like these two. Pinto was the master of the flying headbutt and Scarface impressions and Tuffy was a 6th Dan in some horrible, bone-breaking martial art. I remember one night at the Island in Ilford: it all went off and Tuffy kicked a mugger in the head. It was like watching Bruce Lee in *The Game of Death*. Later on, the police came down looking for the doorman who'd hit the black guy over the head with an iron bar. That sums him up to a tee.

As a team, we became aware of each other's strengths and special talents and functioned like a military unit.

They were looking after me and my mum first and foremost, and then the punters. I didn't have to brief them on what to do and how to do it – most of them had been doing it for years anyway.

With them behind me, I was unstoppable.

THE DOWNSIDE

As you'll have gathered, we did a pretty good job of keeping the aggro away from the party people who just wanted to have a good time but, inevitably, some of the scum got through our safety net.

The second-ever One Nation event at The Island was a case in point. The Island was a tricky place. It had become well-known for fights and murders and we had to be on top of our game. That second night, there was plenty of blood spilt. The worst incident involved a punter getting attacked in the toilets. He came staggering into the foyer with claret pissing all over the place from a shoulder wound. He'd been stood having a piss when some scumbag had gassed him and slashed him, nicking his money while he was incapacitated. They probably weren't aiming to cut his shoulder so, though it sounds ridiculous, the guy was lucky.

Mark – aka R.S aka Inspector Gadget – was just the kind of man you needed in a situation like this. He went into the back office and asked a bird where they kept the first aid kit. *First Aid what?* She looked at him like he'd just fell from the fucking Moon so he went out to his Go Go Gadgetmobile and got his own gear. Back in the venue, he sat the geezer down on the stairs, pulled his top to one side and started stitching his shoulder up. Luckily, the boy was so off his face that he didn't feel a thing as Mark pulled the stitches as tight as he could to keep his shoulder together. This sort of thing was nothing unusual for Mark – he'd been a trained medic in the army and had seen a lot worse in the past – but to the rest of us it was fucking heroic. We were proud of him that night and I knew if we could deal with that so early on, we could deal with anything. Christ, we didn't even have to call the police or an ambulance – we were an emergency service in our own right.

Once the lad's shoulder was sorted, we kept him there while we sent a search party out to find the geezer who'd slashed him. Mark, Albert, Boogie and Billy took on the mission and quickly found the arsehole, a black kid in his late teens who was wandering around looking for more victims. They grabbed him and dragged him over to make sure he was the right guy, trapping him behind one of the glass doors so he could be viewed through the window.

The stitched-up punter nodded. We gave him his money back and I looked at this cunt, stuck behind the door and now looking a lot less fucking arrogant. I wanted to ram it into his face a few times and then kick the shit out of him . . . and as it was my night, that's just what I did. Once I'd had a go, I left him on the floor for the others to finish him off. Four people smashed him up, and then he was picked up and taken through the club, opening every door on the way with his head, leaving his blood on all of them, until he was thrown through the fire doors into the gravel outside, moaning and semi-conscious. He was in pretty bad shape: his head was cracked open but luckily there were no brains in there to spill out, just a lot of air released. The kid who Mark operated on got cleaned up and went straight back into the club like nothing had happened. Amazing. And when we did the next event there, he came back and thanked us. He recognised Mark straight away and was all over him, hugging him and showing us this big, dirty Mars bar scar on his shoulder.

'Look . . . that's what you done. You saved my life, mate!' he was shouting and dancing around.

It was a joy to see someone so grateful because it could have easily been a very different story – the knife could have caught him somewhere else, he may not have made it out the toilet, may not have identified the attacker, we might not have found him . . . there were so many other possible outcomes, it's scary. And with that being our second event, it could have closed us down immediately. I was so pleased he came back and even more pleased that the prick who attacked him didn't.

Life's all about lessons, and I was learning another one in these early days. I loved my clothes and my labels. Don't get me wrong, in the early days I shopped at Mr Byrite, Top Man, Burtons, like anyone would. But once I started making reasonable dough, I'd buy Gucci, Versace, Armani. I went out and bought six of Giorgio's suits one time – I was flash but I loved it. I got into trainers – I had 20 or more pairs at a time, Nikes, Reeboks, Adidas, plus the trackies and t-shirts. The problem is, you can't dress like that if you're promoting raves. It's fine when you're off duty, at a party or dinner or whatever, but if you're kicking fuck out of some mugger you don't want his blood on your £150 shirt, do you? It all crystallised for me as I was rolling down some stairs one night with a geezer who didn't want to be thrown out, and all I could think was, '*What the fuck is this doing to my nice white jeans?*'

You're a scruffy cunt if you're a rave promoter – jeans and t-shirts, a stab vest and some nice heavy shoes. Again, you don't want to be kicking some twat's head in with a nice pair of Gucci shoes on. It fucks the shoes up, it fucks your feet up (people's heads are pretty hard, I can tell you) and it doesn't fuck the twat up enough.

It was like the wild west, some nights. One time, there was a pair of muggers working in tandem. You've got to be really quick and sharp – they swap their caps and jackets to change their description and in the dark with all that noise they can melt away. We lost sight of them, so Jon-Jon set a trap. He gave his gold necklace to this bird and got her to stand on offer. Sure enough, these robbing cunts came up and swiped the necklace. Then we pounced. We grabbed them, Jon-Jon punched them around the club for a bit and then we dragged them up to the office. The idea was to make an example of them and really work them over. We stripped them – they were carrying watches, rings, necklaces, shit loads of money, it was unreal – and beat them till they couldn't walk, talk or see straight. Then we threw one of them back out and we gave the other to Jon-Jon. He had a legendary way with these cunts. He always liked to go just that little bit further with one of them so he'd hobble back and tell his mates what had happened, once his dental work allowed him to speak again.

Jon-Jon tied this cunt up and stashed him in the office. Then, at the end of the night, he bundled him into his car and drove him to Epping Forest. He spent the next few hours torturing the wanker – stubbing cigarettes out on him, pulling his hair out, putting jump leads on his bollocks, that sort of thing. Then he strung him up in a tree for 24 hours before he came back eventually – he forgot where he'd left him, he is quite absent-minded sometimes – to cut the shitbag down and let him stumble away.

My raves attracted a lot of wannabe gangsters . . . and I don't mean a club full of bare-backed, dungaree wearing, Tony Soprano look-alikes drinking water, blowing whistles and chewing gum.

I don't mean any serious, heavy duty, organised crime, either, which might sound odd. There was a lot of money floating around, after all. But if you're a fucking top league villain, yes, you might be able to take 10k off a rave promoter, but that's chicken feed and it will cause a lot of aggravation. People used to say to me, 'Are you worried about getting robbed?' I used to say, 'Look, if they want to come and have a go, let them. We're prepared.' A lot of it was front but ultimately we would have delivered. All my guys were lunatics, they did not give a fuck, they would have had it, no matter who was in front of them. They had their own reps to protect: if someone was taking a liberty with me he was taking a liberty with them.

No, our gangsters were typically rival street gangs wanting to stab each other to death, gangs of muggers armed with knives, trying to steam their way in – every nutcase you can think of under one roof. *My* roof.

So I was obliged to sort it all out. I didn't care what they did at home – they could kill each other if they wanted. When they upset the atmosphere and compromised the safety of my events, then it was a personal threat that I wouldn't back down from.

These big tough geezers would never be on their own, always in a gang and more often than not, tooled up. Bunch of wankers. They'd be searched on the doors, we'd use metal detectors, we'd have their shoes off and still weapons were getting in.

Birds were a big part of the problem. They rarely looked innocent and they seldom acted it. They used to smuggle drugs and weapons in by stuffing them up their fannies. Unbelievable, though some of them did have very loose fannies.

We had to get a woman doorman in – a doorwoman, I suppose – to search them intimately. Once they'd been patted down and were in the club, a few minutes later they'd tap the doormen and say, 'Is it alright if I nip to my car to get something, babe?' And the lads would say, 'Of course.' They'd nod at this doorwoman. 'But she's gonna search you again when you come back in. *Babe.*'

Some of them still thought they'd get away with it. They'd be back five minutes later, we'd run the metal detector over them and it would be bleeping. We'd get them to take their shoes and jewellery off and it would still be bleeping. So they'd be off to a quiet room for a session with the KY and the rubber gloves.

Once the girls started fighting they were worse than the blokes. Have a trawl round on the internet if you don't believe me; there's a few funny sites where they've got footage of birds scrapping. I saw a girl attack her boyfriend at The Rhythm Station one night and had to look away. He walked off from her, she took her high heeled shoe off and smashed his head open with it. There was claret all over the floor and she spent the night in the clink.

Our attempts to keep the muggers, thieves and psychopaths at bay were often hindered by the venue's own security firms. I wouldn't trust most of them as far as I could kick them. It might be different nowadays, but back then they were almost always useless for a number of reasons. First off, they were basically event stewards with a couple of local hardmen in the mix to supervise them. None of them were fighters; they'd have had trouble starting one, never mind stopping it. Secondly, their earnings were minimum wage (or less because it wasn't around when I started up) so they weren't exactly motivated. Would you jump into a knife fight for three quid an hour? I'm fucking sure I wouldn't. Thirdly, on such a shit wage, they'd always be looking to boost it, and they were in a perfect position to let people in back and side doors for a back-hander. Some of them were mates with the gangsters who were operating in the area and would tip them off if any rivals were in the club, or turn a blind eye to any of them serving up. Fourthly, some of them were scared of the gangsters, especially if they lived locally: they wouldn't report any incidents because they'd be attacked in their own home as a result. They were just as much hassle as the trouble-makers: we had to control the venue and its security on top of the three thousand punters and any gangs and muggers who were outside.

One way was to send them a message that would get talked about, like Jon-Jon's torture in the woods.

One night, the lads spotted a couple of twats serving up. I saw them counting money and went over to give them a warning. You know, sometimes a warning can work and it is a lot less hassle than bashing someone up and having to dispose of them.

I said, 'If you're serving up, don't fucking bother, OK? We'll deal with you if we see you doing it again.'

Half an hour later, a punter comes up and says he's just been threatened by two guys who are serving up. Who do we find but the geezer we've just warned, stood with his mate dishing pills out.

Mark went over, locked eyes and told him to walk forward. He did, putting his hands in his pockets as he walked. Not a good move. He might have had a shooter. 'If you take your hands out of your pockets now,' said Mark, 'I'll break your arms before you hit the floor.'

He and Albert walked the pair of them into a side room.

'Right. Take your clothes off,' said Mark.

They just stood there, stunned.

'Take your fucking clothes off. I'm going to search you.'

One of them protested, saying he couldn't do that.

'Well, there's me and 15 other blokes in here that says I can. Now do as I fucking say.'

They started to get undressed and got down to their boxer shorts. Mark told them to shake their pants around so they could see if they were carrying and a load of money fell to the floor. He picked it up and counted just over £1,500. The geezer claimed he was a scaffolder who'd just been paid. What a load of bollocks. Albert searched his pockets and found hundreds of pills.

'OK then, scaffolder. Who's your dealer?'

Silence.

Mark cracked him across the head and asked him again. The geezer told him they were vitamin tablets, not Es. Fucking hell. Even worse, he was a con artist drug dealer – lower than scum. Mark fanned the money out in front of him and the venue security came round to get their cut.

'You're a drug dealer, and you're not even a fucking good drug dealer,' he said.

He brought a lighter out from his pocket and burnt the money – right in front of the dealer's face. The lad started to cry like a baby. Mark threw the burning cash at him and he dropped to his knees, trying to save it.

It was a cool move by Mark. Setting fire to the money sent out a message to the dealers, the police and to the venue security teams. We were not like all the others. We were there to do a job and go home – stealing drug money held no interest for us. All the other door teams could steal if they wanted – and plenty did. If we caught dealers taking the piss, all we were interested in was beating them up, stripping them, burning their profits and sending them home with no clothes. Stay the fuck away.

Over the years that story evolved into an urban myth. We went to quite a few venues where their staff told us the story as though it had happened to them, and each time the money increased. At the last count, it was £30,000.

We did a load of events at Club UN in Tottenham. It was right opposite the police station, which you'd think would mean stress-free events. Ironically, we had a *lot* of shit go on at this place – no one seemed to care that it was next to a cop shop.

The grief at UN started even before our punters had arrived. They would get off at Seven Sisters tube station like lambs walking to the slaughter – literally taking their lives into their own hands. The muggers would be waiting in packs, armed with knives, and they'd just pick them off on the way down. They didn't care how close to the police station or the venue they were. They thought this was their turf and they could do what they wanted. These hood-rat pricks acted like they were in South Central LA, trying to look as intimidating as possible. All of them had the same kind of clothes and the same vacant expression about them, eyeing you up and down like you had no right to be there. That look alone earned them a punch on more than one occasion.

On our second night there, a kid of about 17 came up, close to tears. He'd been mugged on the way to the club and was really shaken up. This wanker had held a knife to his neck – they always threatened to cut people's throats – and demanded money. He had no way of getting home and he was distraught.

I said, 'The guy that did it, is he still around?'

He nodded and pointed the guy out. I couldn't believe this fucker's balls: he was just wandering around, looking for his next victim, bold as fucking brass.

'Wait here,' I said. 'I'll get your money back.'

I watched the mugger casually leaning with his back against a wall, waiting for the another vulnerable victim. I got close up, all casual, and waited. As soon as he made his move, I made mine. He was towering over a young lad, threatening him, and didn't see me as I crept up behind.

As the kid was about to hand his money over, I said, 'Paul! Where you been, mate?'

It took them both by surprise.

'Who's this? Is he a mate of yours?' I asked.

By now the mugger had turned and was eyeing me up and down. With my eyes locked with the mugger, I told 'Paul' to go to the club and I'd join him after I had a word with his mate.

I moved in on him. He was bricking it, though he was trying to maintain his cool. He didn't like the tables being turned on him.

'Give me your money, you cunt,' I said. I was snarling through gritted teeth. I got nothing but a defiant, vacant, spaced-out stare. 'Give me your fucking money,' I repeated. '*Now.*'

The slower his reactions were, the angrier I got. He shrugged and put his hands in his pocket. Now, he either had a knife or a lot of money in there and I wasn't taking any chances. I banged him in the face with a right, knocking him to the ground. It felt fucking good. He was semi-conscious, groaning, and I kicked him three times in the bollocks and dragged him back towards the wall he'd been propped up against earlier. He was on his back, with his head pushed up against the wall. I pressed my foot on to his throat and pushed my weight down on to it, watching his scumbag eyes widen with panic.

I leant forward, and spoke slowly and deliberately so he knew I meant it.

'If I ever see you round here again, I'll fucking *bury* you out in the woods somewhere. Do you understand?' He didn't reply. 'Did you fucking hear me, cunt?' I asked.

He nodded his head as best he could. I took my foot off his throat and before he could move, I crouched down, grabbed hold of his top and punched him in the face again, hard. His head had nowhere to go and smashed into the wall. I let go of him and he slumped down, out of it. I rifled through his pockets for his money and knife, which I put in our confiscated weapons box for the police to have. I stood up; he was still sparked out cold and I couldn't resist one more kick to the bollocks before making my way back to the club. When I crossed the road and looked back, he was still in the same position.

My mum was comforting the young lad when I got to the club. I gave him his money back. Two other kids told us they'd been mugged and that added up to the remainder of the bundle.

Club UN was bad for mugging – it never let up once.

We had another occasion where three white kids came in, almost crying because they'd had their tickets and money nicked by three black guys. Their names were on the tickets, names that no black council estate kid was likely to be called. When the scumbags got sick of mugging people outside, their plan must have been to come in and get the people they missed earlier. So after half an hour, in they walked. I was on them immediately. I cut them off before they reached the cash box and asked them their names. They stuttered and stalled and asked why.

I grabbed their tickets and said, 'Well according to these, your name is Rupert, yours is Alexander and yours is Giles,' I said, pointing to each in turn. 'No need to look so shocked, lads. We just need to search everyone who comes in, that's all. It's a random thing, licence requirements. We've just picked you out – it'll only take a minute.'

I led them upstairs to our torture room; they were nervous, and didn't want to come, but they knew they had no choice.

Inside the office, a couple of the lads were waiting to greet them.

My tone changed. 'Right, boys. Take your clothes off without one word. The first person to speak without answering a question gets his tongue cut off and stuffed up his arse.'

Not one word was uttered as they took their clothes off.

'Hands behind your heads and kneel on the floor.'

We took a bag of surgical instruments around with us

wherever we went – just for show really, to make them as scared as their victims were. I made sure they got a good look at these tools. Then I waved a roll of bin liners at them.

'You are not getting out of here except in bits in plastic bags unless you're very lucky,' I said. You had to really scare the fuckers, give them a taste of their own medicine.

When they were kneeling, we got behind them and stomped them down to the floor, grinding their faces into the carpet with our boots. Their pockets were emptied and all their personal stuff was destroyed – designer sunglasses smashed up, trainers burnt, phones crushed. We took the belts from their jeans and whipped their backs till they bled. They were crying in pain and fear by this time, and the venue manager must have heard because he walked in. 'What are you doing? The police station's just over the road.'

We told him what happened and why we were doing it and he left us to it. We kept the muggers ID and told them if they came back to any of our clubs, we knew where they lived and we'd pay them a visit that they really wouldn't like. They must have gone to the Old Bill, because later that evening, two cops arrived.

'These three kids reckon that you tortured them and smashed their stuff up,' said PC Not Interested, pointing to a trio of very sorry looking fuckers with blood encrusted bodies and torn clothes standing behind him.

I went through our routine answer. 'They were mugging people, we stopped them, they were going to attack us and we clumped them before they could. Anything other than that is a lie.'

'They also said it was a racist beating. Is that true?' he asked.

That was when Gary stepped in. 'Do we look racist to you?' he said. 'I'm the same colour as they are. Those three young boys are a disgrace. If I saw them mugging people I'd have given them a clump myself, officer.'

'Look,' I said. 'They're bad lads. Why don't you search their car?'

One of the police officers went off to have a look in the vehicle. He came back with three flick knives. They ran a radio check on their names and found they'd just been released from jail for robbing an old woman in her own home. At knife point. Lucky cunts. If we'd known that from the start, we would have taken them for a drive out to the forest and they might never have come back. They'd certainly have needed a few months to get over the beating we'd have given them.

They even used to try it on after the kids had left. One day, a load of my punters were robbed on a train half an hour after we'd finished. Ten black geezers got on and steamed through, doing everyone. Not much I could do about that, even if it made me angry.

I know it sounds like I'm being racist, just talking about the black muggers. There must have been white muggers, and black victims, but the truth is, nearly every single mugger we ever dealt with either inside or outside the club was black. I'm not a racist – loads of my mates, on and off the scene, were and are black. A lot of my security team were black, and we're still good mates. They'd tell you the same. These fuckers worked on the basis that all the white kids believed that the black kids would stab you for no reason. Even after being mugged, half the victims were too scared to say anything and too scared to identify them in case they saw them again on the street or at another rave and got seriously hurt.

We'd say to them, 'Press charges. You can get them done,' but they weren't interested. That was the kind of ready-made fear the muggers had, so there was the psychological advantage from the start. They all came from the worst areas imaginable – the kinds of places where you only live when you are at rock-bottom, where drugs and crime were a way of life. Our events were stuck in the middle of all this, so they just had to take a knife out and earn. Personally, for all that they had tough home lives, I didn't understand them. What's the point in mugging some kid for 20 quid, or breaking into a house and stealing a DVD player? They're

30 quid new and you'll only get a fucking tenner for it. If you're that fucking desperate for money why don't you go and get a job instead? But then you can't lie around all day smoking crack and puff, I guess.

We didn't *have* to get involved, we didn't *have* to listen or give a shit, but we did. If kids wanted to come to my event to hear music that I put on for them, they had every right in the world to do that. I liked our punters, they were a good laugh, young, well-dressed and into having a laugh. These hoodie wankers had no right to take their money from them and I despised the lowlife cunts.

By the way, it wasn't like I wanted all this shit. Yes, I've always wanted to stand up to bullies, ever since I got bullied at school. Yes, I put bullies, muggers, grasses and burglars on the same level: the lowest people on this earth. And, yes, I got satisfaction out of giving some thieving cunt a clump and getting a victim's money back for him. But I hated having to do it, really. I just wanted everyone to have a great time and go home happy.

Sadly, the world isn't like that. With 3,000 people all in one place, all with money, watches, necklaces, designer clothes, it was too tempting for the scum. They knew most of the kids were young, or weak, or off their nuts, and they could turn them over.

WILL THE REAL TERRY TURBO
PLEASE STAND UP?

ONE Nation had been running for a couple of years and it was going really fucking well. We were getting known on the scene as one of the best promoters around. Our events were almost always rammed and my pay packets were getting fatter and fatter. With all that came a lot of jealousy and bullshit.

In these 15 years of madness and mayhem, I've been described as, in no particular order a gangster, an arsonist, a psychopath, a womaniser, a thief, a fighter, a practical joker, a great shag, a drug dealer, a grafter, a flash bastard, a racist and a con man. There's loads more. I agree with one of them one hundred per cent, and maybe three others if pushed.

People I dealt with in my line of work didn't see me relaxing at home, as a family man, a provider. I was taking care of my mum and my Nan, and I'd got a daughter by now, Jade. She'd been born after a relationship I'd had with her mum, Sarah. Sarah was a raver I'd hooked up with, a really good-looking girl who loved life. We'd known each other for two or three years, seeing each other a couple of times a week, and we decided to have a baby and move in together once she got pregnant. Well, she got pregnant very quickly and we started living together. Fuck me, talk about mistakes. Living with someone is so different from going out with them, and we were at each other's throats from the start. We had nothing in common and basically wanted to kill each other. We split before Jade was born – they now live on the south coast and I see Jade regularly, which is cool. I don't like the fact that Jade comes from a broken home – Sarah did and so did I, so maybe the patterns repeat themselves.

Anyway, people didn't see that side of me. I supported a lot of charities, too – mainly Arthritis Care, because my mum and Nan both had arthritis, Cancer Research and the World Wildlife Fund. But people didn't see that side either.

To them I was Terry Turbo: a tough guy who probably dealt drugs and spent most of my nights getting off my head till 5am.

Probably it was partly my own fault. Those close to me knew the real me, the lads I worked with knew my sense of humour, my temper and all my quirks, but in a cut-throat business, I could never afford to let my guard down in public. Having human characteristics would be a sign of weakness; it had to be business every waking hour.

What else did people say about me?

That Terry Turbo geezer is a gangster.

I'll go into this a bit later. I did hang round with a lot of gangsters, it's true, so I was automatically in danger of being tarred with the same brush. Suffice, for now, to say I was not, I am not and I never have been one myself.

That fucking Turbo geezer is an arsonist.

Probably one of the maddest things I've been called. Some offices got torched and the geezers who owned them thought I was the culprit.

It would have been funny if it wasn't taken so seriously. Rumours like this can be very damaging, so I phoned one of them up to put the record straight.

'Don't go around spreading things about me, OK? I have no interest in burning your offices down. If I was bothered about you, I would have set fire to you, not your office.'

After a pause for thought, the guy said, 'Hmm . . . I suppose you're right.'

'I fucking know I'm right, mate.' I added. 'Why would you think I'd do something so shit to you?'

They got embarrassed and lost for words, and ended up saying that the thought had just crossed their minds.

Fucking hell – the thought crossed *my* mind that it could be an insurance job, but you didn't hear me telling people that.

Truthfully, it was fuck all to do with me. I leave this sort of thing to the idiots who believe real life is a gangster film. If you go down that road of fucking people over, they'll always know someone who is capable of doing it to you. Or they could just throw a grand in each and get you shot. The risks outweigh any gain, so I'd rather walk away than get involved. Life's too short to fuck around like that – it's a lot easier to get on with people than to make enemies. (Incidentally, they turned out to be a couple of good geezers, who eventually bought the One Nation stable off me, so they obviously realised I was innocent).

Terry is a flash bastard.

Guilty. To an extent. I liked my clothes, off-duty, as I've said. I liked my cars, too (to look at – I can't fix the fuckers). The gold Allegro passion wagon was long gone, and the BMW 320i, too. I'd gone through a 328i (28k brand new, I thought I'd made it then), a Jeep, a Range Rover, a 5 series Beemer, a Jaguar XK8 with R7BAD on the plate and loads of others. I *knew* I'd made it when I bought my first Porsche. Everyone was always banging on about them, so I went to the garage and said I wanted a bright red one with the GT3 kit on it – I half thought about sticking the GT3 badge on it, but if I'd wanted one that bad I'd have bought one – with the wooden interior, beige leather everywhere . . . it was a 100k motor by the time I'd finished speccing it. A fucking load of bollocks, really. I put 15k down and had the rest on the strap with a balloon at the end of it. Six months later, it was finally ready. I remember looking at it, with the TURBO number plate on it, and thinking, I've arrived. Ridiculous, looking back, but I was a young bloke. I climbed in and the sales guy got in the other door. He started going through the spiel, how to turn the wipers on, where the lights were and all that bollocks. After about two minutes, I said, 'Look mate, do me a favour. I'm going for a drive, I'll work it all out later.'

I remember driving out of the garage and people were staring at it. A great feeling, it was so cool. I knew I was losing money just driving away from the garage, but I've always been a sucker for that new car smell.

So – flash? A bit, yes. But not like a total twat.

It was the DJs who really got the hump about my cars, particularly the Porsche. Some of them were right up their own arses – they thought they were talented, when really they were just one step up from some cunt playing Shakin' Stevens at a wedding in Clacton. They all had BMW M3s and didn't like me driving a better car than them. I was just a promoter, after all. They didn't know that I was doing a dozen other things to make money – I wasn't a one-trick pony – and this would always fuel other rumours as to where my money was coming from. It was all *bitch-bitch-bitch*.

But fuck them. I earned money and liked spending it. If I saved it all, I'd be called a tight-fisted bastard, so I was never going to win. And I've never forgot where I came from and money has never changed me. I'm still the same Terry who lived with his mum in a council house in Camberley.

Terry Turbo is dishonest.

I was less than honest once or twice. We did an event at the Coliseum in Vauxhall and over-sold it. We'd got rid of all the tickets with a couple of weeks to go, demand was still strong and we could sell tickets on the door for £25 apiece. The venue held two thousand people and I knew we could get away with another 800 inside. If we pulled it off, we'd make another £20,000 on the night – very good money. Six like that a year, and you're really laughing.

It was a challenge, too. The manager – Fishy Lips we used to call him because of his massive lips – was so anal about the amount of people we could have in, it really used to irritate the life out of me.

I got the printer to make a load of spare tickets with duplicate numbers on them and some others in different colours which I could claim were guest list comps if I got rumbled – the idea was to muddy the water as much as possible. I gave the top doorman five hundred quid and told him to underclick the amount of punters coming in so Fishy Lips wouldn't be any the wiser. Sure enough, two thousand people turned up on the night and we sold another five hundred on the door. It was almost impossible to move inside – absolutely fucking sardined, with more queuing up to get in. Including the guest list, we were around a thousand punters over the limit, and with mum in the cash box, skimming like a plasterer on speed and filling her handbag up with tickets, we were home free. Or so I thought.

Once I'd done the wages books and everything was running smoothly, I always liked going upstairs for a bottle of beer and chill out, if possible. On this night, I could just about get through the front door and no further. Fishy Lips fought his way through the crush to get to me. 'Terry,' he said, a look of panic on his face. 'Something is wrong. There are too many people in. I want to check the tickets.'

I told him he must be mistaken. We checked with the geezer 'clicking people in'. He'd done the business: officially, there were only around 1,700 in.

But old Fishy Lips wasn't as stupid as he looked. He put his fin down and told us we couldn't let any more people in the plaice (no more fish puns, I promise) and told us to refund the punters still outside.

He knew *something* was going on but had no idea *what*. As a compromise, we let pre-bought ticket holders only in, and had to turn everyone else away, which was a shame.

On Monday, the phone rang. It was Fishy Lips. He'd been right all along. Something, other than his lips, had been very fishy indeed. He said, 'You've conned me once and you will not con me again.'

I played innocent. 'What d'you mean? We only had two thousand in all night,' I said.

'Terry,' he said, 'I've just watched the CCTV footage on the door and re-clicked everyone in myself. You're fucking lying.'

I had to admire his determination. He'd sat for five or six hours and counted nearly three thousand people on a little black and white monitor. Imagine the fucking headache that would have given him. Fair play, send that man some paracetamol.

'I could lose my bloody licence over this,' he said.

Squirming, I said, 'It must have been your door staff. Seriously, nothing to do with us.' With it being a phone conversation, he couldn't see my nose growing.

He wasn't happy, but he couldn't prove it was down to me and we parted at stalemate. I walked over to the fridge and took out some humble pie, which I kept especially for occasions like that. Greed can hit us all. I was making so much, I thought, *Why not go for an extra few grand?* In my defence, where I came from, you never know when you'd be making your last tenner, let alone your last ten grand.

At most clubs, you could get away with it. The doormen were on around £150 tops per night and would happily turn a blind eye to a few hundred extra punters if there was a drink in it for them. Everyone was driven by money and head doormen were always slippery fuckers. Picture the scene – you know Dazza Doorman, you're out with a couple of birds you want to impress, and you give Daz the nod so he takes you all to the front of the queue and walks you in for a 20 quid backhander. You're be over the moon because he just made you look like Henry Hill, Daz is happy and his missus is happy. Ten or 20 people out of 3,000 aren't ever going to be noticed, so there's at least two hundred quid in his sky rocket. I always told my firm that they could let a few people in for free, as long as they weren't clicked in.

Another night when we ran the ticket scam, it all went tits up, and I don't mean any old tits up – this was colossal, fucking Jordan's tits up. We were crammed in to the Adrenaline Village with three thousand inside and at least another three thousand outside. Fuck! We locked the front doors and the crowd weren't having any of it. We let the ticket holders in and there were still another two thousand or so outside – all the bad-boy Garage kids who thought they were the dog's bollocks. They took the side fire doors off within minutes and it was fucking mental trying to control them. Gary the Gooner was in his fucking element. It took him back to his terrace days; he was smiling as he was battering them to fuck. The riot police came in the end and the crowd fucked off. It was a close one – absolutely mental. Probably the worst riot we ever had.

Terry's on a short fuse . . . he just goes off on one.

Well, I've been known to, especially in my younger days. But lots of times when it's been on the cards I've held back. For instance, one time, a company came along who started leaning on every promoter you could think of. It was a record label and as DJs played a lot of their music at events, they started taxing promoters for putting all the tape packs out with their artists on.

It just so happened that the guy who had the record label used to run with a well-known football hooligan firm, so any deal he struck with you would be as fair as it was ever going to get – a sort of *give me some money now* kind of deal. With tape packs, promoters would record all the DJs from the night, have them turned into tapes and sell them. When you considered intellectual property and copyright laws, the record label was well within its rights to get paid. In this scenario, it was the promoters who were taking a liberty by using someone's work to make money out of. No permissions were ever sought and no contracts signed. Thinking about it logically, if we were in their position, we'd be doing exactly the same thing.

The first promoter on their list was stung for £20,000 and, after a few other promoters were summoned, we got a call asking us to step into their office. As long as I had a hole in my arse, I wasn't going to give them anywhere near 20 large. We thought about taking a couple of the firm down to the meeting – showing we knew people and could take them on *may* have been an idea . . . just not much of a sensible one. If we were going in for a row, then OK, a firm would have been handy. In this instance, we had to be tactical rather than aggressive. It was pointless starting a war just because they asked to see us.

We went into the meeting all humble and showing remorse. The record label geezer kicked off by calling us worse than shit for using his music on our tapes.

I said, 'If you don't want us to play your records at our raves, then we won't.' It was a bit of reverse psychology because that was the last thing he was expecting to hear. With us producing tape packs with their music on, we were promoting their records, so it wasn't like they'd see no return. That's how punters bought records.

The deal we arrived at was to pay them for the last few tape packs and to negotiate each deal separately with every future release. Being the biggest promoters in the business really helped our case – we could have just paid them a stack of money and banned their records from our events if talks went down the swannie. It proved that by talking about it as reasonable businessmen, we could reach a compromise.

Terry's a womaniser.

Again, guilty in my early days, before I settled down. If some beautiful 20-year-old bird in a bikini top and hotpants comes up to you and asks you very nicely if you'll please take her in the back office and fuck her to pieces, it's very hard for any red-blooded man to say no. As One Nation got bigger I did say no, because I was too busy. But the temptation was always there. I remember I went to a Desire event and then on to an after party in Tottenham, in a pub in the middle of a right moody council estate. I'd had enough, but I'd also had a few too many drinks (there's a Kanye West song in here somewhere!), and there was no way I could drive home. I thought I'd go and sit in the car and this bird who used to work with me said she'd come and keep me company. So we're in the car and I'm trying to go to sleep, but she just kept talking and talking. In the end I said, 'Look, babe, I'm really tired… can you shut the fuck up.'

She just grinned, bent down and started giving me a blow job. Well, it kept her quiet.

I was sat in this car, getting sucked off in broad daylight and I looked up and there was a cop car driving by really slowly.

Luckily, he didn't see what was happening and she carried on.

One presumes that awful Terry Turbo is a drug dealer.

Being a young guy with money, it was obvious that I was a drug dealer or some other sort of criminal. Wasn't it?

I've always loved earning money and spending money – they're two of my main vices. Let's face it; you can't beat wearing the nicest clothes, driving a good-looking car, being as comfortable as possible and in your own fully-furnished, well-designed top-notch gaff with all mod cons. But I worked every waking hour to make a legitimate living. I remember a few years back. I'd moved up in the world, property-wise, and was now living in a lovely house in a much sought-after part of the country; the kind of place where lawyers and retired property developers live. The kind of place, as it goes, that dislikes anyone who isn't middle-aged and didn't make their money in a conventional way.

In moves Turbo, none of the above, non-traditional, non-conformist, non-impressed by the *I'm better than you* brigade. My neighbour was an oddball. It bothered him that he'd worked all his life in his highly-paid job, only for someone like me to move in next door. He'd be constantly watching what I was up to, riddled with envy each time I changed my car or got a new number plate. Because I wanted to extend the house and was applying for planning permission, I thought I may as well befriend him for a bit in case he became difficult.

My good neighbour looked around, all shifty-like, and then started in his lowered voice, 'So, how do you make your money? Is it drugs?' he asked.

I stared at the silly cunt, and raised my eyebrows. 'If I was a drug dealer,' I said, 'then having a £100,000 Porsche Carrera 911 with a £25,000 TURBO number plate on it wouldn't really be the smartest move, would it? Don't you think I'd have a bit of a lower profile?'

Why the fuck does he need to know how I earn my money? And why didn't he ask, 'Is it because you are the biggest rave promoter in the country and are savvy enough to have several other ventures going?'?

Young. Successful. Drugs. Say no more – everyone thinks that – unless you look like a footballer, not a football hooligan.

* * *

With One Nation going well, the market was obviously there to expand.

My mate Jason Kaye used to play for us at Club UN all the time – he'd DJd for me way back at Rhythm Station as Top Buzz, which was two DJs – Jason and Mikey B – fronted by an MC, Mad P. They went on to become one of the biggest acts in the country. Mad P used to laugh, saying they ought to be called Two Blacks and a Bubble, because Jay's Greek. Jay used to spend all his money on records – he could predict the next trends, know tunes before they were popular, he was destined to work in music. He'd be in a club and ask the DJ to play his current favourite tracks, the DJs wouldn't even have heard of them. They'd gone their separate ways in 1997, with Mikey B going on to join the Dreem Team at Radio One and Jay carried on making music and producing.

We weren't particularly close but we'd kept in touch since the Rhythm Station days and (literally) bumped into each other at a mad party, The Black and White Ball, at the Royal Albert Hall.

I remember him saying, 'Terry, this Garage thing is going to be massive, man!'

Garage music was emerging on to the scene in the mid 90s and got its name from the Paradise Garage club in New York, 'Garage' originally being an American term to describe the records that were played at the club. It's basically like drum'n'bass meets hip hop and R'n'B. People like The Artful Dodger (featuring Craig David) brought Garage into the UK charts, and then there was the dirtier, darker stuff like Dizzee Rascal.

I said I'd give him a call and we talked over some ideas and ended up deciding to set up Garage Nation. It was to be the start of a great friendship and a great business.

I couldn't lose focus on One Nation so I roped in a mate, Murray Taylor, to work for me and Jason. I also pulled out of the flying side of things now, and I gave that business to Murray, for free. I just couldn't devote the time to it any more.

I also closed down *The Scene*. Other mags had started up so I was working my arse off in a venture that was slowing down because of an over-saturated market. There were times when people didn't advertise or if they did they didn't pay the bill, and it reached the stage where, some months, we were struggling to break even. In the mag's heyday, it had brought in two grand a month – not likely to worry IPC Magazines, but fucking brilliant when you consider its humble beginnings. But I didn't see the point in losing money for a few months on something I could see had been on the decline for a while. It had served a purpose and had already outlived its shelf life. If it wasn't for *The Scene*, I reckon it would have been harder to break into promoting and would probably have taken me a lot longer to make the transition. Because it was an extra way to increase my contacts list and my knowledge of the industry, it helped that natural progression.

With Garage Nation now taking up a lot of my time and attention, it was great to have Murray alongside, helping us along. He was a good geezer to have around – I didn't need to be on his back hassling him all the time and, likewise, he wasn't always asking me ridiculous questions with obvious answers. It was Murray's job to make sure the flyers and distribution all ran smoothly and that the tape packs went to the shops and all money was collected every week. It was a cushy job in a way because there was a formula we'd sorted with One Nation. All Murray had to do was follow suit and be honest. He'd been working with me for three years, so if any problems cropped up he knew me well enough to speak up. The job was even cushier when I got him a car. Fuck me – I'd gone from driving company cars to dishing them out. You always see an initial change in someone's appearance as soon as they get a good job. Murray used to be a window cleaner, so it was great to see him starting to do well for himself at last. He smartened up, looked well and started spending money on his missus. Spending too much money, it seemed. Soon he'd got himself another motor, a house and was going on exotic holidays. I knew we were making money, but our names are Terry and Murray, not Brinks and Mat.

It didn't add up and I smelled a rat. A big fucking rat. One that looked like Murray Taylor and sounded like him every time it squeaked.

I'd had my suspicions at an early stage because I noticed that the tape sales weren't what they used to be. Each month, they were around 100–150 light, and the envelopes of cash were starting to get lighter and lighter. There could have been a slump in the market, but . . . Nah. Bollocks. Could there fuck have been a slump in the market. Selling tapes to mad-for-it ravers back then wasn't a market that slumped.

While he was away in Thailand on another trip overseas, I had two weeks to suss him out properly. I took over his job while he was away, purely for snooping purposes, and didn't let on to anyone what I was up to. The first day was typical – people coming to the house to pick flyers up and heading down the office to sort things out. A couple of lads arrived, so I helped them carry the boxes to their car. They had loads of tape packs in the boot.

'Did you buy these, fellas?' I asked, all casual.

'No, Murray gives us those instead of wages.'

Things that make you go *hmmm.*

I went back to the office and called in all of the guys who worked for us. Eventually, we had just over 30 people in and all of them were being paid in every method you can think of other than money – mainly freebie tape packs. Even worse, some were buying packs off Murray at full price and he was keeping the money.

It turned out he'd nicked around 150 tape packs per event, covering the losses up by claiming we'd had returns which he'd sold cheap, or that we were being supplied short orders. Over those six months it meant that he'd stole £20,000 from me.

It was a kick in the nuts. It wasn't the money going missing that bothered me – it was the friendship and the betrayal of trust that got to me. The fact that a mate could do that without a second thought really fucked me off – and it was like he couldn't give a fuck whether I knew. He was mugging me off.

I called him up on holiday and told him to come round and see me as soon as he got off the plane – as soon as he touched down. He came straight round with his fucking suntan on my money.

I said, 'I want the keys to the office.'

He looked pretty surprised, but he handed them over.

'You are no longer part of Garage Nation, One Nation, Turbo Promotions or anything else,' I said. 'You're getting fuck all else from me, you cunt.'

He had the cheek to ask why, so I told him *exactly* why. The tan drained from his face immediately. He thought I was going to take his head off, and if I'm honest, I'd considered it. But stopping his income would hurt him for a lot longer. Thieves think they are entitled to everything for free so I was leaving him with nothing. I was calm and in control, I didn't want to lose it.

'You watch me over the next few years,' I said. 'You watch how I go and remember that you could have been a part of this.'

I showed him the door and he was gone. He'd got off very lightly because he knew what I am capable of. In another way, he hadn't. He'd mugged himself off, really. He could have been earning for another ten years if he wasn't such a greedy, thieving cunt. You know, a tape pack here and there for his own entertainment would not have gone amiss. I wouldn't have minded at all. But 100 to 150 packs a time to sell and keep the money was taking a liberty.

Money is a strange thing and it does strange things to people.

The whole industry was crawling with people like that. I'm honest – I paid everyone what I owed them, unless I had very fucking good reason not to. I'm not a con man and couldn't have survived all this time if I was; when you rip people off, they never forget it and they *will* get you back for it, one day. I assumed everyone else was like that, which was a bit naive.

People would rip you off, or just fuck you around, as soon as look at you. The company we used to get our tapes from was a case in point. They started delivering our tapes late – anywhere up to four weeks, which just wasn't good enough. Punters would go to the rave and want the tapes from it to relive the moment (or just to try to remember it in some cases). In four weeks' time, they're not going to give a flying fuck about the event, and would have been to a few more in the meantime. I found out other promoters were getting theirs into the record shops within a week, which meant we couldn't compete. Some of these other promoters were getting their tapes produced by the same place as me so I phoned the company up to find out what was going on.

'Why do they get their tapes within a week and I have to wait three or four weeks to get mine?'

He told me it was because I got credit. Was this fucker for real? I said it didn't matter if I got credit or not, I was still paying for them and I was still ordering more packs than anyone else. Because they weren't getting my tapes to me in time, they weren't selling and I had a fucking load of them I couldn't get rid of, sat in a warehouse. He saw sense. He knocked over £30,000 off the bill, took all the old tapes back that he admitted he fucked up on and promised that he would turn our stuff round a lot quicker in the future. Result.

True to his word, that's what happened and all was hunky dory until six months down the line when he started doing it all again.

I phoned him up again. 'We've already had this fucking

conversation, and you've already given me a refund,' I said. 'You've delivered my tapes late and now they are not selling again. We're going down the same route and I'm not going to fucking pay you for them.'

His reply was the same – he was sorry, gave a refund, blah blah blah.

A year and a half later, he pulled exactly the same fucking trick *again*. I couldn't tell if he was just stupid or had a bad memory. Or both. He phoned *me* up asking for money. I hadn't paid about fifty grands-worth of invoices and he wanted his dough.

I went through the whole story as calmly as possible, like I had before: as long as he kept delivering a late product that I couldn't sell, I wouldn't pay for it. As a compromise, I collected all the tapes that I had, gave them back and said I'd pay the difference. I had around eight thousand tapes and they were charging me five quid for each one including tax. OK, eight thousand times five quid is £40,000 that they'd be knocking off the bill. I owed them £50,000, which meant that, with the deduction, I owed £10,000, give or take.

He picked the tapes up, left a credit note for eight grand and said they were only paying a pound for each tape. Now, that is a huge difference – instead of me owing him £10,000, he wanted £42,000 – absolutely ridiculous. I refused to pay and said I didn't have his money, never would have his money and he'd never get a penny from me in the future. If he hadn't been such a wanker in the first place, he would have got paid. Fuck him. I had enough reasons not to pay, I think . . . forty two fucking thousand of them.

All this was going on behind the scenes. At every Garage Nation, there was still all the shit to deal with the same as One Nation. Only it was much fucking worse.

At One Nation, we had to contend with muggers with knives. With Garage events, guns were the big problem. We got all the fucking street kids whose idea of fighting was to shoot the place up – most of those who came out planning to cause aggro came armed. It all seemed to be to do with 'respect' and status and how cool they thought they looked. It didn't help when you had Garage acts who'd made it into the top of the UK charts in the news for their association with violence and guns, and all the twatty American stars posing around with their fucking 9mms and Uzis.

The Garage kids were dangerous, not because they were tough – they'd never fight you – but because they were arrogant little cunts who just could not be told. You'd tell them they couldn't come in, they'd start yelling about how you were dissing them and, next thing you know, they're waving a fucking pistol in your face. Sometimes they didn't even need an excuse: a lot of them truly believed that they owned everything they could see and we were *on their patch*. It was a dangerous fucking combination and one which caught a few people out. Across the country at Garage events, punters and doormen were dropping like flies. My mate Felix – another doorman who worked for us from time to time – got shot in the leg by some kid in a queue to get in a club. It wasn't one of mine, thankfully – he was working elsewhere. Him and this kid had a minor argument and the kid shot him. Completely fucking unnecessary – a stupid argument with some dickhead could cost you your life. We had metal detectors and shit, but the available technology was in its infancy and we just couldn't stop every gun carrier. All we could do was our best – and jump on any fucker who even mentioned guns – because we knew they weren't just making idle threats. When they said they'd be back to shoot the place up, they'd do just that. If we allowed them.

Obviously, we did our best to keep the guns out – metal detectors, careful searches, the lot. Some still got past us. Incredibly, sometimes it was through the DJs: they started smuggling guns in for their mates. Un-fucking-believeable. They'd hide them in their record boxes and hand them out inside.

I found out when one of my mates came up to me in a club and

Then and now. Boxing as a 15-year-old - great training for the challenges ahead
- and suited and booted 15 years later.

My Team were legendary and top men, every one. Among them were *(above)* Billy and Boogie and *(below)* a bearded Felix, Jeremy Bailey and a sharp-suited Adam Saint.

Gary Gooner *(l)* was a total gentleman, while Warrior terrified everyone: both were fantastic members of the Team. Below, Boogie, Raymond, Dave Courtney, RS and Albert with me and mum at her wedding to Don.

And this was what it was all about - thousands of ravers off their heads at One Nation and Garage Nation events...

...if you can spot the few muggers in among the happy clubbers, you're half way to joining the Team.

The spoils of war. Best Club Promoter 1997. And *(below)* I'd come a long way since my mum's council flat and a clapped-out Ford Capri, too.

We had the strangest people come to our parties. Here, my mum takes a ticket off the Queen while I meet Alexander O'Neal, a musical hero of mine, backstage. One of these people is a 'Fake', by the way.

My foray into the gangster fraternity, through my friendship with Dave Courtney, brought me into contact with some top faces. Above *(l-r)* at a charity night, I rub shoulders with Johnny McGee, Baz, Joe Pyle, Big Albert Chapman, Tony Lambrianou and Mickey Pugh. All great guys, but the No1, for me, is my close mate - and 'dad' - the legendary Wilf Pine *(below)*.

said, 'Look at this,' brandishing a handgun. It was a tasty 9mm Glock automatic.

'How the *fuck* did you get that in?'

He told me and I went fucking mental. Just like all the other fuckers who stepped out of line, I made an example of DJ Gun Smuggler: had him beaten the fuck up and thrown out on his arse, with his bird. The muggy little prick. In hindsight, we should have let a few rounds off at these twats each time they played a shit tune just to show them how dangerous a gun in a club could be. They thought they were the coolest thing in the world, that the world revolved around them. Knives, powder, pills – anything that wasn't allowed, they'd try to bring it in.

There was this geezer called MC Sparks who smashed a wine bottle across some girl's head one night. Pleasant chap. He was lucky to get out of there in one piece because he was in serious danger from everyone. Even the venue security had their sleeves rolled up. Just when everything had calmed down, the bird went to her car and came back to the club with a gun, waving it around threatening to shoot him. *A fucking bird!* The police were called and she got nicked. She was lucky, really. With the amount of weapons in there, someone could easily have blown her away before we called 999.

We had a fucking serious set-to at The Sanctuary in Milton Keynes. A gang of about 20 or so guys from Manchester arrived. Supposedly, they were part of some Manchester gang – one of the country's most notorious young black firms, responsible for dozens of shootings and deaths up north in 'Gunchester'. They could have been Kool and the Gang, for all I cared. There they were, all in their hoodie-homeboy baggy clothes, giving it all that shit about 'respect' and saying they didn't want to pay at the door.

Well, it's not a fucking charity event, boys.

'I don't care who you are,' I said. 'There is no way you're coming in here unless you pay.'

In the end, they grudgingly handed over the wedge.

'Right,' I said. 'Now, if you come in and fuck around in my

club, you're going to get hurt. Respect us, and we'll respect you.'
Sorted.

About an hour later, the punters started leaving and I mean *big* numbers of them. It was only 12 o'clock and the rave was going on until six in the morning. Something was up. I nosed around and found our friends from Manchester causing trouble. They all had their hoods up and were picking random fights – pathetic stuff like kicking people up the arse and then punching them in the face when they turned round.

There was no choice. They had to be stopped. I called venue security over and told them I wanted these lads thrown out. The house team shit themselves and just refused: we'd have to do the job ourselves. No problem. They were causing aggro in my club and now they were going to get smashed up. I got my boys together and approached them. One of them got right in my face and was telling me – OK, was *starting* to tell me – how it was. I steamed straight into him, sending him flying with my first right. I hit him with all my anger – no cunt could have taken a punch like that and stayed upright. As he went down, I smashed him with a left-right combination. He lay on the ground, sparko, and I stamped on him as I walked towards his mates, twisting my heel to make sure he'd feel it when he woke up. Right behind me, the lads were snarling like a pack of Kamikaze pilots, knowing they were down in numbers but going in regardless, knowing they'd come out on top, spreading enemy claret all over the floor.

You'd think a big posse like that would have been a bit tasty, wouldn't you? Sadly, for them, they weren't. We bashed a few of them randomly as they scattered, then linked arms to charge and force them out the fire doors down the far end of the club. On the way, we were still clumping and kicking them. It was a bit of a struggle, but the lads all looked like they were enjoying it – and they *were*. The likes of Gary and Jon Jon towered above everyone, heaving them forward and bringing their fists down on them like sledgehammers. With Jon Jon pushing you, you fucking move; you have no choice.

Having a proper row in a club is surreal. It's disorientating anyway, so when you can't hear any noises, it makes it all the more bizarre. You'd hear tiny snippets of shouting and swearing here and there – and you'd look over to see the lads pounding into some geezer's face. With all the lights and lasers and strobes, you saw everything in slow motion. Each punch we threw was a leveller with no time for hanging around. Bang . . . next . . . bang . . . next. We knew they weren't going to come back in a hurry.

Scooby was outside protecting the back doors, so once they were thrown outside, he gave them a slap too and then Animal and Warrior started grabbing them, arms and legs, and flinging them into this huge ditch by the grass verge outside – the One Nation crew's mass burial site. There was blood, teeth and groaning, squealing bodies everywhere.

You always find some humour in this sort of thing, and seeing all these geezers piled up outside was the laughter we needed. They were all either knocked out or close to; we'd done all 20 of them in five or ten minutes, just the eight of us. We had a chuckle and then walked back into the club. Job done. Then one of the boys on the door radioed through.

'Tel,' he said. 'They've all gone over to their cars. I'm watching them now . . . they're putting body armour and balaclavas on . . . fuck me, they're pulling guns out. They look like they're getting ready for a war.'

Bollocks. Fool and the Gang were coming back in a hurry after all.

They surprised me, I must be honest. I thought they'd fuck off after the kicking they'd had. But what a pisser: now they wanted to shoot us for finishing something *they'd* started. Fucking brilliant. That was the mentality of these geezers.

A few of my boys were usually prepared for this kind of situation: when it's mine or my mum's safety at risk, I had to take all the right precautions, and you need the ultimate tools handy if it all turns really bad. I never asked who was carrying because I didn't want to know. The only details I needed were that *someone* would be ready, willing and very able.

And then it hit me. Earlier that day, I'd had a call from the manager of the club warning me about being tooled up. There had been allegations that someone from the venue security staff was dealing drugs and the police had been down a few times to search them. If they suspected anyone, you couldn't refuse to be searched, so there were no bats, coshes, gas, dusters . . . nothing.

We locked the doors and called the rozzers in. And believe me, they were there like shit off a shovel, arriving inside two minutes with an armed response unit, tooled up like Terminator 7. They must have known something would happen that night. They rounded the gang up – all stood there in balaclavas and bullet-proof vests – and searched them. They couldn't find so much as a water pistol – it turned out one of them had sped off with all their guns on a motorbike. The police let them go, which I found pretty fucking amazing despite the lack of guns. Did they think they were going paint-balling? They knew the gang and what they were up to.

The head of the police unit came over to me.

'Look,' he said. 'These are a serious firm. We haven't found any guns now, but you can bet they'll get them back as quickly as they got rid of them. Your card's marked. I need to get you and your team out of here as quickly as possible.'

What a fucking downer. The event had to go one without us – the first and only time it's happened.

The Old Bill told us they'd drive us out of town. They waited for us out the front while I got everyone together for a head-count. Because a lot of the boys were time-served ex-military, all a bit naughty and had a few quid to play with, there were a few top of the range Mercs and Range Rovers and BMWs. The coppers all stared open-mouthed as we drove our motors round from the back. Their jaws really dropped as we got kitted up in flack jackets, night vision goggles and encrypted radios. Our gear was more advanced that theirs.

We were given an armed escort out of there, me sat in a Range Rover in silence with my mum, looking out at these police cars at either side thinking, *Has it really come to this?* Once safely out of the area, the police left us to continue on our own. We were still uncertain. Out in the front of our convoy was a mate of mine in his brand new Astra van who called me up on the mobile.

'I'm really worried, mate,' he said. 'I'm sure they're watching and are going to fucking ram into us.' He added a lot more F words in there too. I tried to calm him down, reassuring him as best I could without worrying my mum.

I'd got it all a bit wrong, though. He didn't give a fuck about the danger, it was his paintwork that was worrying him. 'I'm only insured on third party,' he said. 'I'm worried that if they try to ram us and I ram *them* that I won't be covered.'

If he wasn't so serious about it I would have pissed myself laughing on the spot.

I said, 'Look mate, if anyone tries to ram us don't worry about the insurance, just fucking smash them off the road and I'll buy you a new car, alright?'

It was priceless. And it certainly took my mind off the gang on the way home. I had visions of him trying to swap insurance details with some Manchester mobster while dodging bullets. Why couldn't people just have a fight and sort their differences out on the spot? Those geezers, or gangstas as they'd love to be called, had tried it on and got fucked up. End of story.

After that incident, we made a conscious effort to make sure that if someone stepped out of line, they were smashed up to the point that they couldn't walk to their car to get their guns. Our mistake with these twats had been in only knocking them about a bit. In future, if we let anyone off so lightly, we might not live to regret it.

We ran parties at the Rex in Stratford. It was a rough shithole, to be honest: Jon Jon used to say to me, 'Why the fuck are we doing this place again? I fucking hate it.' So I used to send him off to have a look around the loudest rooms where I knew he'd hate it even more. The first time we did The Rex, we had around 25 kids mugged on their way in. It was eating me up inside that these cunts had got away with it. I drove home that night furious with them and myself for not being able to do more. The next day, I drove back to Stratford and around all the side streets and hiding places in the area and worked out exactly where the muggers would be hiding at the next event. I doubled my security for that one and told the guys just to wear their normal clothes. We were all over the place, at the train station, hanging around the streets trying to blend in, walking past casually. As soon as they approached anyone . . . crack! They hit the ground before the kids even knew what was about to happen. No one got mugged that night – not one person. The police had plenty of complaints from would-be muggers, though.

One night, we had two gangs in from Birmingham and Nottingham. The Brummies were from the Burger Bar Boys – the crew who shot Letisha Shakespeare and Charlene Ellis on New Year's Eve a while back – and the Nottingham lot were some other equally fucking dangerous firm. For some reason, they can't come out for a night, take a pill if that's their thing, or chill with a few drinks, get laid, have a dance and go home. They have to start fucking fighting. They began by carving each other up outside and then carried it on inside, for hours on end. Eventually, we located them and threw them out. The Nottingham lot were trying to get back in but because the doorway was so narrow, they could only get in in single file so we just battered them, one by one, as they came in. There were bodies left all over the place and we ended up carrying a fair few of them out into the car park.

Most of them eventually fucked off, realising they'd bitten off a lot more than they could chew. But as four of the geezers walked away, one of them said he was going to his car to get his 'machine' – ghetto-speak for gun. As soon as we heard that, we all ran after them. They pegged it to their car, knowing that if they got to it first, and got their hands on the weapon, they'd have the upper hand.

It was a vivid fucking few minutes, and I can relive it to this day.

They manage to get inside and lock the doors. The driver's trying to get the key in the ignition but his hands are shaking so much he can't. The passenger is scrabbling about under his seat, looking for the fucking gun, and the boys in the back just look petrified and keep yelling and shouting at the driver to get the fuck out of there.

We surround the car and start smashing it up with bats, Maglites and coshes. The bonnet comes up, so we do the engine, ripping out every lead we can see. Now they're trapped in a car that looks like it's been in a wreck and won't start. One of the boys puts the windscreen through with a Maglite, someone else does the rear screen and Mark leans in and gasses them. Things just got even worse for the poor fuckers: now they can't see or breathe, they're choking and they've got to come out. A few times they try to open the doors; I can only assume they think getting a kicking outside will be a relief compared to what's going on inside – but we lean on the doors. The passenger finally gets his hands on the gun and looses a shot off, maybe two. But it's ripped away from him by someone leaning in. We batter the absolute fuck out of them: by the time we decide they've had enough, the car, which had once been a brand new Mercedes, is unrecognisable. So are the geezers in it. They're slumped over, unconscious and covered in blood. If you'd passed by, you'd have thought the car had just been hit by a train. The car's parked outside a gay club at the bottom of the road and a little crowd has gathered outside, watching. We're like, 'Nothing to see here. Go back inside please,' and we hurry back to the club.

Once inside, I got a bit paranoid. We'd really fucked up the four guys and I started thinking we'd maybe overstepped the line, that they might actually be dead or dying. I didn't want my mum and bird around if there was any armed comeback – or we got arrested – so I decided to get them out of the place without telling them what had happened. I had to walk my mum past the car to mine. The four are sitting, semi-conscious and moaning, on the kerb, and the Old Bill had arrived and were trying to talk to them.

My mum's eyes nearly popped out of her head. 'Oh, look,' she said. 'I wonder what happened there?'

'Dunno, mum,' I said, keeping my head down and hurrying her past. I didn't want the cops roping me in. Amazingly, they never put two and two together and the four boys from Nottingham never tried coming back.

Other firms weren't as severe on these cunts as we were, and they paid the price.

We were due to put on a rave at the Island in Ilford. Two weeks earlier, the venue door team got hold of some muggers and threw them out. As they did, one of the scum turned and shouted 'I'm gonna come back and shoot you, man.'

To which the head doorman responded, 'Yeah, course you are. Fuck off, or you'll get another clump.'

Trouble was, the guy was serious. He went to his car, got out his gun, walked back and opened fire, calm as you like. He did his whole clip: one of the bouncers was shot dead and the head doorman got hit in the arm and spent a week in intensive care.

He turned up, arm in a sling, at our night a couple of weeks later.

I took one look at him and said to my lads, 'See that, fellas? Anyone who misbehaves here tonight, we just smash them up so bad they can't do nothing.'

The head doorman went mad. 'I got shot last week, you cunt,' he started saying. 'One of my guys was killed. You do that, they're gonna go and get a gun again.'

Trouble was, he was upset because he knew I was criticising him in front of his team. It nearly started a bit of a war: all the venue's doormen were going, *'What you doing? You're gonna get us all shot again!'*

They started edging forward, we started edging forward and there was a bit of a stand off.

I said, 'Look. If you'd done your fucking job properly the cunt wouldn't have been *able* to come back and shoot anyone.'

For me, no way would I let the guy walk away after making threats like that. It was enough for him to go to hospital, and I don't think that's unreasonable force. You had to take it seriously and a two-week-old corpse in the local morgue was the proof.

Warrior held up his hands. 'Listen, guys, he's right. If someone says he's going to shoot you, you don't just let him fuck off.'

They could see the sense of what I was saying, and it all got defused. I understood their boss's attitude, a bit. He was emotional, his mate was dead, he was in pain from his shoulder, he probably felt a bit of guilt about what had happened. But at the same time, we didn't want to be in that situation ourselves.

Funnily enough, that night we caught a mugger who started making threats. We beat the shit out of him . . . stamped on his ankles and arms – I mean, *really* stamped – and broke his nose and jaw: he couldn't have gone and got a gun even if he'd wanted to. He had his driving licence on him so we took that off him.

'Right, you cunt,' I said. 'We know where you live. If we ever see you again we're gonna come round and do you. We're not playing games.' He got the message.

It wasn't just gangsta punters who wanted to know. I got a call one day from a mate of mine telling me to watch my back because of some Yardie guy. I was intrigued, as you'd expect. We were doing raves over at Brixton Academy and it turned out some Brixton firm was going round telling everyone I was paying them off so they didn't come and ruin my nights. My blood reached boiling point in seconds . . . it was red mist time.

I got my mate to pass a message on to the head of this firm. 'Gather your fucking boys up and meet me at the Academy. I'll bring my boys and we'll sort this out.'

Not too long after, I got a call from the guy. I got straight to the point, 'When are you coming down for your envelope?'

He denied all knowledge of the 'protection racket'.

'I won't be paying you or anyone a penny in protection money,' I said. 'Anyone tries that with me, I'd rather pay someone ten grand to kill them and bury them somewhere. I've got the money and I will do it. I'm letting you know exactly where I stand on paying people protection money.'

He knew I had the connections and the money to do it, and this was probably not the sort of talk he was used to coming his way.

Would I have gone that far? No. But it's like playing poker, you have to be able to play your best hand *and* know how to bluff people to win.

With Garage Nation, it was a constant fucking battle with muppets and their guns.

I phoned the police to arrange an armed response unit to be parked outside our venues. It may have seemed like an odd request at first – until I told them who I was and why I wanted one. I offered to pay for it all – whatever the cost, I didn't care. I mean, you can't put a cost on the safety of a few thousand people, can you? I was the one who brought it all together and I saw it as my responsibility – it wasn't just the punters, there was the venue staff, venue security, DJs, MCs and my firm. I know the venue security don't count as real people, but I still didn't want them to get shot while I was there. I'd probably have to mop the blood up.

The police told me they didn't provide that kind of service for anyone.

I asked what I should do if someone came to a club and started shooting it to pieces. They said I should call 999. In 1990, Public Enemy did a tune called '911 is a Joke' – they should have released a UK version. If some fucker pulled a gun, by the time we called the police and they arrived, the shooter would be long gone, unless we disarmed him and got someone like Jon Jon to sit on him to keep him there, or he happened to get shot by someone else.

It pissed me off, to be honest. The police didn't want to bother themselves with helping to protect people, or my livelihood. But they'd waste no time in shutting me down if people did start getting shot.

GOING GLOBAL WITH GARAGE NATION

Before long, Garage Nation was as big as One Nation, and I hit on the idea of franchising the brand – very similar to my old mates at McDonalds, where I'd worked all those years ago.

The idea was, I'd get other promoters around the country to put nights on for me under my name. They'd have to conform to certain standards – I couldn't have any old twat running a night as One Nation or Garage Nation – but as long as they gave the punters what they'd come to expect from us, a good night with no trouble, we could do a deal.

It worked like a dream. On a given weekend, there'd be One Nation nights in Leeds, Manchester, Birmingham and three or four other towns. I got paid for the right to use my brand and someone else worried about promoting it, managing it all and clumping people for stealing wallets. Any problems that arose on the night were nothing to do with me. I could be sat at home having a crap, and I was still running a load of raves. It took all the worry and the stress away from me and was a genius idea, if I say so myself. It was the perfect set up and so simple to put together. All I had to do was arrange the flyers and pay someone 50 quid to travel up with a banner, give out the flyers and keep their eye on things. They got their petrol money, a night out, and were paid to fly it, which came to around 70 quid all-in. All their drinks were covered by the venue and they could take as many mates as they wanted. Another perk was these places were crawling with seriously good-looking women. Always. Whoever took the job that night was the promoter of One Nation or Garage Nation – they were the face of the organisation and had all the birds throwing themselves their way. It was fun for everyone and I was always keen to work on a jobs for the boys basis. If it was their bag, I'd arrange for one of them to DJ, too, earning money for that on top.

I either arranged an upfront fee – half paid upfront as a deposit, the rest paid to our representative on the night – or did a quid per head deal. Mind you, the upfront fees were OK and if I was paid by the head, well, three thousand people meant three grand in payment. So I was laughing, especially if we had five or more running a night. The local promoter would put out anywhere between 10,000 and 20,000 flyers and it gave us a name nationally, because it looked like it was us who'd done it all.

We took it all over: Scotland, Wales, Cardiff was always good, Swansea and Leeds were always good, Leicester too, but a bit rough, Manchester – fucking nightmare but good. All the northern cities were the ones that kicked off most of the time. No idea why. It was a lot different to the clubs down south, where the violence was more predictable, somehow. The northerners were just mad as fuck – it's the only explanation.

Once I realised how different the people were in other places, I thought there's no fucking way I'm going to drive up to Manchester, carrying three grand around all night and then drive home. I may as well draw a target on my back and carry a big neon sign saying, 'Rob me' – though, surprisingly, no one was ever robbed. In fact, we had no away losses whatsoever. If we took it to a predominantly black area, I'd make sure a black geezer did the job, and vice versa in a white area – on the basis that gangs are less likely to attack people of their own colour.

I had backdrops made to go on the tours. These were fucking huge banners with One Nation and Garage Nation logos on. I started with just one, and ordered more when we were busier – at a few hundred quid a pop, they weren't too expensive and once they were in place on the night, it meant we owned the event. We could have them spread out all over the country on the same night and the punters didn't know I was sat at home with a glass of wine relaxing. Tours meant that I could be in six places at once and not many other people can claim to have done that.

Though we didn't take our own security firm to club tours – we were relying on the venue security if any aggro did kick off – a lot of the boys played the promoter role. Having someone like Gary Gooner as an away-day promoter, I knew the company was in safe hands. A good thing about the tours was that most of them were held in universities and you didn't get half as much aggro as you would in a normal club. That's not to say there was never any grief. One time, we'd licensed the name out to a club down in Kingston. My Mate Terry Fisher was one of the team inside the event when it all kicked off with a load of cunts steaming through the venue. Terry and a couple of the other door team started dealing with them, and got split up – Terry on one side of the fire doors, the other two boys kicking fuck out of five of the muggers outside.

Terry's trying to get out through the door to give them a hand but it's blocked by the weight of one of the bouncers. He's trying to get the door open when he gets rushed by a dozen more of the gang. One of these cunts tries to stab him with a foot-long carving knife – it's so hot Terry has taken off his stab vest – but Terry manages to make him miss and traps the guy's wrist under his own arm, meaning the knife's out of the game for a moment or two. The others start punching fuck out of him: Terry can't keep the knifeman trapped forever and he really thinks he's about to die. Suddenly – Terry says it was like the cavalry appearing – Gary Gooner, Gerald, Billie and CJ, one of Gary's mates, come of nowhere and save the day. They massacre these dozen cunts – one them ends up with a broken arm, the rest are battered to fuck.

Gary and the other boys weren't even working there that night: they just happened to be in the place. They saved Terry's life. That was what the team was like.

Eventually, the tours took on a life of their own, to the point where I had to employ an agent to deal with it all. They weren't huge money makers individually, but the cash soon mounted up – to around £60,000 in a good month – and our name was getting exposure up and down the UK. I'd still be putting my own events on in London, so it was pretty hectic with that and flying and doing everything else at the same time.

We also started going abroad.

We did some legendary Garage Nation events in Ayia Napa, but the first was a disaster. A geezer called Illayas who owned The Emporium paid us a load of money to come over, but turned out to be a complete psychopath. He met us off the plane and I was with a couple of geezers from my firm, and Richard (of McDonalds fame) came along, too. He drove us to the hotel like any self-respecting Formula One driver would. Drivers are crazy over there at the best of times, so the last thing we needed after a flight was to get into a car with the James Dean of Cyprus. We were in the back, hatching a plan to kill him before he managed to kill us.

In the club on a night, he'd come up to me going, 'Terry . . . Terry . . . Terry . . . whaat do you want to dreenk?'

The usual, of course. Champagne and lots of it. He kept tearing these little drinks vouchers from a book to give to us and in the end we just took the whole book off him and drank the place dry. I told him we needed some more and he was hysterical. 'You have drank eet all,' Terry, he said.

They were great nights and we had a right laugh, but it turned a bit sour in the end. We found out he was doing tapes and CDs without us knowing and would make a lot of money from eet, so we had a meeting and asked to be wedged up. Illayas had no more money, so we had to go and see his old man in some moody hotel. Even when we counted the money out, it was still short, so we had to wait until they found the rest of it. Slippery fuckers. We were lucky they paid up in the end, really. If they'd brazened it out and told us to fuck off, there wasn't much we could have done about it. We couldn't have got heavy with him, because he had hundreds of guys to call on. We couldn't have gone to the law, because they were probably on the take from him. We'd have had to smile and walk away.

Working in Ayia Napa, and Ibiza, was not like working at home. In England, if you had a row with someone, you could sort it, one way or the other. You were known, you had your team as back-up, and – though there was always the risk of some 17-year-old cunt blowing you away because you looked at him wrong – the likelihood of a serious player, a promoter, a club owner or whatever, doing anything really stupid was minimal. Over there, on these islands in the middle of nowhere, it was a different story. You were on your own, thousands of miles from home, in a foreign land where everyone knew everyone else.

Say you fall out with some geezer called Javier, or Stavros. You're using their club, you know you had 2,000 in but he says you only had 1,200 and he shows you the clicker to prove it.

What can you do?

A mate of mine, a sensible, proper geezer, went over to Ibiza to do a regular night in this club and the club ripped them off. They had an argument over it, and my mate lost his cool a bit. He was demanding to count the money, the club owner wouldn't let him. Eventually, my mate said, 'Listen, I've got people in London, I can pick the phone up and they'll fucking come and take you away, you cunt.'

And the Spanish guy was, 'Yeah? Well, you ain't in fucking London now, son, you ring who you like.'

That night, my mate's door was kicked in – *by the Old Bill*, for fuck's sake. They dragged him out, smashed the shit out of him and told him to go home or he was going to disappear.

And there were several English promoters who *did* go missing over there – people were thrown over cliffs, or found with their arms chopped off. There were lots of stories about people being driven out into the country, shot in the back of the head and thrown down wells. If you were lucky, the police kicked your door down, 'found' a bag of Es and you went to jail for three years.

Thing was, there was serious, serious money to be made – millions of pounds a month was being generated by clubbing on these islands, and – in Ibiza – millions more through the drugs trade. Ayia Napa was essentially drug-free – you could find it if you really went looking, but the local people don't like drugs and the police make serious efforts to get rid of dealers. In Ibiza, it was *everywhere*. You couldn't move ten yards without being offered coke, speed, Es or grass. If you wanted heroin or crack, you'd have found it, easy. When you have that kind of scene going on, you know there are serious, heavy duty criminals behind it all.

The lesson for me and Jay from the Illayas fiasco was, if we were going to do Garage Nation in places like Ibiza and Ayia Napa, we needed to be in with the right people. In Ayia Napa, that mean working with the Mallas brothers. They were Cyprus's version of the Kray Twins, a pair of guys who, with their dad, owned the water park, all the clubs and a lot more no one really knew about – basically, unofficially, they owned the entire Ayia Napa side of the island. We managed to get ourselves hooked up with them, and they invited us out there to talk. The first eye-opener was when they had us walked off the plane and into a limo without bothering with all that passport and customs shit. Obviously, they were seriously connected. The next was at dinner. At the table was the Mayor, the Chief of Police, the old man, the brothers and us.

OK, we weren't going to mess about with these guys.

Wherever we went on the island, we got the best table in the restaurant, the best champagne free of charge, people fawning over them and us and doing whatever they could to make us feel welcome.

We tied up a deal to promote in their clubs and worked with them for three years, doing Pasha, Emporium, the Ice Club and Pzazz – all the best places on the island.

We negotiated flat rates for the Mallas's to use our brand

and expertise, much like we'd done back home, just on a bigger scale.

This was the best way forward. OK, you didn't make as much money as if you were handling the whole event yourself. But if you were promoting it yourself, you weren't watching the ship back home, for starters, and you were also putting yourself on offer for all the local criminals, and the bent Old Bill, to come and have a go at you. You'd need a massive team out there just to watch your back, and that all costs money. With all the fucking stress and potential danger that entailed. If you had a flat rate, there was no danger of a fall-out with the locals, because they knew what they had to pay you up front and it was all agreed. Even if the club had a bad night, we'd still get the same money. Plus, they paid for everything – to get all the DJs over, for their visas, flights and villas, their living expenses, and every other headache you'd end up having to sort – and we just sat back and relaxed. The deals varied from a grand to a few grand a week, which was a very nice earner over three months of the summer clubbing season. On top of that were the tapes and CDs and t-shirt deals – it was all sweet.

The club managers would let us know which DJs they wanted, we'd phone all the agencies and say that we had whichever club in Ayia Napa from Thursday to Sunday, from whichever date in June to another date in September, and get them to send us a sheet with a list of which DJs were available. We'd pass that on to the club, and get them to pick who they wanted when and where, and we'd book them up. That was as stressful as it got.

One club we never got that I always wanted was Moulin Rouge. It was like Stringfellows, a strip bar full of gorgeous women. There was one bird who was Russian, absolutely stunning, and could only speak in broken English. So I put on the Turbo charm and she came back to the hotel with me and spent the night doing unspeakably disgusting things with me. It was unbelievable. The next morning all the lads were waiting for me in reception because I was always the first out the door for breakfast. We came down the stairs and she still had all her stripper gear on that she was wearing the night before – thigh high boots and all that caper, and I was grinning like the Cheshire Cat. She sat herself down on me with the lads and started playing with me through my shorts in front of them. I called a cab for her and then she gave me her number and said I'd call.

My mates were like, 'She can't just give you a ham shank in the hotel in front of us!'

'Well,' I said. 'She just did.'

It was fucking hilarious. No one could take their eyes off her.

It was great while it lasted, Ayia Napa. We were the highest paid people there, put up in the best hotels and wined and dined in the best places. We'd go out for a couple of weeks each season, on holiday effectively, and spend our time sunbathing, drinking and shagging birds.

It all started to go a bit sour towards the end of the 1990s. There were so many promoters desperate to break into the place that they'd do it for next to nothing, or even for free. Nights were opening all over the place, which diluted the market. In the UK, people might have a club they go to every month without fail. When they're on holiday, and there's 20 different places on one night, there is no loyalty. If a desperate promoter is prepared to go over there for a couple of quid and a few beers as payment, the clubs are getting their night for a fraction of the money. It got to the point where it wasn't worth it for us or them.

Just ahead of our last season out there, we met up with a Cypriot geezer called George. He seemed like a nice guy, another 'businessman' who wanted to talk. There didn't seem any harm in it so when he invited us to come for dinner at 'the island's best feesh place' with him one night, we agreed. We drove out of town and gradually left the bright lights behind, heading out into the countryside, through the little villages. Eventually, even they stopped and we were in the middle of nowhere.

'You sure we're going the right way for the restaurant,

George?' I asked, as we turned left off the road and started down a deserted, bumpy track.

'Oh, yes, Terry,' he said, with a big grin. 'Ees down thees way.'

I started thinking about those promoters getting thrown down wells: this was smelling seriously fishy before we even got there.

I said to Jay, 'He's going to fucking murder us.'

It was the only possible outcome – there was no way anyone would set a restaurant up out here. Even wild animals would get lost in this. We had no tools with us and no backup. If he was carrying, we were fucked.

Jay had been enjoying the ride up until then. Suddenly, he went on a paranoid one.

'Fuck me!' he whispered, all bug-eyed. 'D'you reckon? What the fuck are we gonna do?'

I was just thinking about twatting George and trying to do him before he did us when he bounced round a bend and there was the restaurant. The swarthy cunt was on the level. I'd never had seafood as good in my life, and I haven't since.

George was like some old school wise-guy, talking slowly and deliberately, like a cross between Paul Sorvino, the *Goodfellas* boss, and Yoda.

'Next year, Garage Nation I want. Ayia Napa. I will pay you £30,000 now.'

'You want to pay us £30,000?' I asked.

Jason was going, 'Let's take it, man,' and I wanted to. I *really* wanted to. He was talking Cypriot money as well, so it would have worked out at a lot more than 30 grand UK. But Jase had already agreed a deal for the following year with the Mallas brothers, and our word was our bond. Unfortunately.

George was disappointed but he understood. He said the offer was on the table if we ever wanted to take him up on it. As it turned out, we probably should have – next year, the Mallas's fucked us around and by the time we went back to George he was sorted with someone else.

Around the time we started in Ayia Napa, we decided to try

our hand in Ibiza. For those who've never been, it's much the same, only more 'English' – there's more drugs, more sex and more violence, with fish and chip shops and burger bars instead of the nice restaurants you found in Ayia Napa. It was also the biggest rip-off on the face of the earth. I'd been there as a young raver and didn't enjoy it much: when you've spent 500 quid to get there, and it's 25 notes to get in a club, a fiver a drink, you can blow a grand in no time. At that stage, I couldn't afford to be spunking that much dough up the wall and I was always amazed at how they got away with it. But, on the plus side, it's a clubbers' paradise: they've got the biggest clubs in the world, with the likes of Manumission – 15,000 people every night, every week – and Amnesia, which does the same with 6,000 punters. My take on Ibiza was, if you just want to get off your head and not sleep for seven days there's nowhere better. The state you see people in is fucking hilarious. I remember one time having some lunch with my then missus, just sitting there laughing at two lads just totally monged out, off their faces, in the restaurant, in the middle of the day. You can get seriously messed up, fucked up, blown away on drugs out there if you're not careful. The sun's shining, loads of Es and whizz and puff and you don't sleep for a week. Next thing you know, the CIA are in your telly and they're coming to take you away. In moderation, with the odd pill here and there, a few rum and cokes, you can end up dancing your tits off and shagging a load of birds, which is great.

When I went back as a promoter, and all my flights, hotels, clubs and drinks were free, it was obviously a fantastic place.

We started off doing Summon – only a 1,000 capacity night, but it went well. The following year we ended up moving up in the world and went on to a 3,000 capacity club called Eden, opposite Es Paradis. The guy out there who we did all our business with is a legendary, mad Scotsman called John Davis. I have never met anyone as funny or as switched on as John: he can drink anyone under the table and be up at 8am the next day to run his empire and believe me, he has an empire.

I had some legendary nights out there. We'd be in the clubs all night, and then doing some great after parties at places like Space, a great club with a really good atmosphere. It's right by the airport, and it's funny as fuck watching spaced-out ravers duck as the planes come in. We met Puff Daddy – as he was then – in Space. He was surrounded by bodyguards but we thought, Fuck it, you don't see someone like him every day, so we approached him. What a cool geezer he turned out to be. We had a good chat, he gave us some free Sean John hats and T-shirts – before he'd even launched the brand proper – and asked us if we'd like to party with him at Pasha.

'Er,' I said. 'Can we get back to you? We may be a little busy on Friday.'

Did I fuck. We grabbed his hand off and it was a fucking unbelievable night. He knew how to give it the massive large – he didn't just have a few tables, he had the whole of the upstairs of Pasha and that is a very large amount of square footage. There were hundreds of people there, with a couple of bottles of Cristal at £900 a pop on each table, a huge lobster buffet and waiters badgering you with cocktails all night long. Me and my mate did six bottles of Cristal between us, which was a bit of a tactical error. We ended up feeling a bit under the weather and staggered home instead of to the after party on his huge boat. That would have been mental; I'm sure we'd have had our brains shagged out by some P Diddy groupies, which wouldn't have been a bad thing. He doesn't hang around with too many mingers.

We also got followed round by Loaded in Ibiza – a TV series on Sky, which followed six promoters around for the summer. They came down to Eden and then the cameras came round on a night out with Tony Hadley from Spandau Ballet. In another episode, the So Solid Crew flew over and spent a night being abused by John Davis after he took them out on a massive brandy and champagne bender.

Back home from my first summer out in Ibiza, I'd obviously not had enough sunshine so I decided to book myself a holiday to

St Lucia for a week with my bird. I'd discovered the joys of good hotels and expensive holidays – even though I always resented paying a fiver for a glass of Coca fucking Cola (eventually, I got over this. I got to the stage where I'd got it, so I'd flaunt it. This might not last forever – I could lose it all and go back to the council estate, be working in a shop. I have no qualifications and I can't actually do anything, except maybe sales, so I might as well enjoy my Coke, even if it cost 10 times what it ought to, because I didn't want to go on holiday to places where it only cost 50p).

I got on the blower to Murray Beetson from Dreamscape, another promoter and a good mate I'd met through the scene and always bumped into at after parties and stuff. He was a character, Murray – a 6ft 2in, long-haired, funny cunt with a busted nose, a big grin and a love of silly hats.

'I'm knackered, Tel,' he said. 'I've just booked a holiday to St Lucia . . . I need a break.'

'Fuck off,' I said. 'That's where we're going. When are you going?'

'Next week,' he said.

'*Fuck off*,' I said. 'So are we.'

'Fuck *right* off,' he said. 'What day?'

It turned out we'd be there at the same time and staying in the same place. Uncanny, eh? That's just what our girlfriends said.

On our second morning there, I opened the patio doors to the balcony, had a stretch and admired the scenery. What a beautiful place. As I sipped an ice cold beer, I heard, 'Oi . . . Turbulence!' It was Murray on the balcony directly above me doing exactly the same thing. 'Fuck *offfff*!'

Through the week we went out all the time and had one of the best holidays I'd ever been on. Murray had me in stitches – an absolute comedian – to the point that I couldn't finish my meal one night. What a fucking scream.

After the holiday, one of Tyson's fights was on the following week. We arranged a get together in a country pub just outside

Northampton, where Murray lived. The idea was, we'd have a few sherbets first, then go to Murray's to watch the fight. I drove up with Chris Brown in Chris's new Merc and they were all on the way to being pissed when we got there at about 10pm. Murray was buzzing like mad because he'd picked up his own new car – a Porsche 911 – earlier that day. He'd been banging on about it on holiday and when we left to go to his place, he asked Chris to go with him.

'Come on, Chris,' he was going. 'get in with me. It's a fucking lovely motor.'

But Chris didn't want me driving his car, so Murray asked me.

'No, you're alright, mate,' I said. 'I'll follow you with Chris.'

He grinned and shrugged his shoulders, and gunned the motor, speeding off like a lunatic, with his wheels spinning and gravel and rubber flying everywhere. It was pitch black and he took off up this hill: in the dark, with his lights blazing, it looked like he really *had* taken off.

I turned to Chris and said, 'If he doesn't slow down, he'll fucking kill himself.'

We set off after him and saw him disappear over the crest of the hill. The next thing we saw was a huge flash of light. We got over the brow and found carnage all over the road. He'd hit a Granada head on. The Granada looked like it had been squashed in a crushing device – you know how big they are, well, this one was the size of a Mini – and was covered in blood. There was glass and bits of bodywork everywhere, smoke and fumes and absolute chaos and the poor people inside were dead – probably killed instantly, getting hit at that speed.

We went over to Murray's Porsche. It was fucked up, but not that bad, weirdly, and he wasn't there. I said, 'He must have been pissed and he's on his toes to avoid the Old Bill.'

Then we looked up the road and we saw him lying in the middle of the Tarmac 20 or 30 yards away, where he'd been thrown from the car.

I ran to look at him. It looked like he was asleep – there was no blood. Murray was always wearing pristine, brand new clothes and he had a new Stone Island jacket on, which was ripped.

I said, 'He's going to be so fucked off about this jacket.'

Looking back, it was obviously a bit more serious than that, but I guess I was in shock. The whole scene was calm, a nice country road with these two wrecks, ticking as what was left of the engines cooled down, and all this violence and death. It was eerie and confusing.

We didn't move him, we just rang the cops and they came with an ambulance. We followed him to the hospital and stayed there until the early hours, but there was nothing that could be done. A load of family members were at the hospital and everyone was distraught. He'd just got engaged to Stacey, they were having a house built, they were going to get married . . . and now it was all over. Everything got taken away that night. Their life together was just about to start. It was fucking horrendous.

The funeral was a fucking horrible thing. Murray's family were there on one side of the church, all nice people, and there were all these fucking idiots from the rave scene on the other side.

At one point, two degenerate crackheads – a DJ and an MC – actually had a fight in the church. That is the kid of scum we're talking about. I stood there, watching them, and saying to Chris Brown under my breath, 'I'm going to cave those cunts' heads in, I'm gonna put them in the fucking ground.'

I was so angry that they had come and disrespected my friend's funeral: a guy who'd given them work. I don't care what differences they had, they should have sorted them down the road.

Chris said, 'Terry, don't do anything, walk away, forget it, 'cos if you start smashing them up you're as bad as they are.'

He was right. But neither of those cunts worked for me or anyone else ever again.

Stacey tried running Dreamscape without Murray. We all wanted it to carry on because it was his legacy to music: he'd been at the top of his game, and untouchable as a promoter. Keeping the organisation going had to be done immediately or it would crumble, and it needed someone who would hit the ground running, but it was too difficult for her to manage everything. She didn't need the extra stress and before long she sold it on to a geezer called Steve Foster. He didn't have a lot of success – he tried setting a few things up with other people and within just over a year, was in danger of running the whole thing into the ground.

That was when he approached me, 'Terry, you know what you're doing... do you want to buy Dreamscape?'

By then, we were on top of Drum'n'Bass and Garage, and Dreamscape was all about Hardcore and Techno stuff. I thought about it and thought a lot about Murray. We'd done an event together in the past – it hadn't made a lot of money but I'd always admired him as a promoter. I couldn't let it all just die away. So me and Jason bought the company, hoping to save it from being ruined. After about four events, having it for less than two years, I couldn't see a future in it at all. I was too close to it and there were so many personal memories. I thought the company was cursed – Murray had died, the next geezer couldn't do anything with it, we couldn't make it work . . . something wasn't right. Steve knew someone who wanted to buy it, so I was glad to sell it on. The same happened – the events couldn't piss on anything that Murray had done in the past and, not long after, it was put to bed.

Dreamscape should have ended when Murray died. No one with all the best intentions in the world could have filled his shoes. Murray *was* Dreamscape, and that was the only way it could have been.

GANGSTERS, PRANKSTERS AND RAVING LUNATICS

Terry's guide to being a gangster:

1. Befriend a load of gangsters and start hanging around with them.
2. Start believing you're a gangster, too, and do silly things for them that you don't get paid for.
3. Get shot dead, or seriously hurt, or end up in jail.

My guide isn't really as comprehensive as it should be. But based on my experience of most wannabe 'gangsters', it's the guide that most of them seem to have followed.

Of course, the real ones tend not to go around telling people they're gangsters until they've retired, and the above guide does not apply to them.

It's not about a salary, it's all about reality says KRS One in *My Philosophy*. My philosophy is slightly different. It has got to be about both. I'd have been a raver but I wouldn't have *worked* in the rave industry if it wasn't for the money – in fact, sometimes the money wasn't even worth the aggravation though I'd never have admitted it at the time. I was making money out of something I loved, so I couldn't just walk away from it.

The bottom line when it comes to being a gangster is that you hang around in a gang. The gang will be involved in organised crime in some way – that's the basic framework that we all know from reading the books and watching the films about them. We've probably got two main perceptions of gangsters – archetypes – both media-generated.

Exhibit A, Your Honour:

The American phenomenon born out of Prohibition – the smart-suited type immortalised by De Niro playing Al Capone in *The Untouchables*. These are the old school gangsters. You've seen the updated version in *Goodfellas* and quoted Joe Pesci's *Funny How* scene to your mates in the pub; you've watched them in *Casino* and wanted to run your own place in Vegas. We all have. No wonder kids think that crime is glamorous . . . Henry Hill in *Goodfellas*: 'Ever since I was a young boy, I always wanted to be a gangster.'

It was all about the cars and expensive suits and the women it attracted – young geezers making stacks of money and enjoying themselves. Of course, they were breaking the law, but they didn't care, did they? And we followed their stories because we were intrigued by them. They were bad men, but we didn't exactly despise them.

The British version started with Ron and Reg Kray. They weren't the first, but they are the ones we remember because they became icons of the '60s. Their look was influenced by the likes of Capone and George Raft, and you read about them in *The Profession of Violence* and in the thousands of other *my dad knew someone who knew someone who knew the Krays* books. They were folk heroes and were feared at the same time. The Richardsons were a lot scarier, although the Krays were the most famous. This was the first time we saw criminals mix with the rich and famous, film stars, pop singers, even royalty – they became the first celebrity gangsters and manipulated the media very well. There aren't many people who don't think of the David Bailey photograph with Ron peering over Reg's shoulder when they think 'Kray'.

The thing I admire about the old school gangsters and the

Mafia is that they had honour. They'd sit down and discuss problems and at least try to sort it out with words before resorting to bullets. Their whole ethos was about knowing people and influencing via a friend of a friend network. They always had style and an image that sits in time – and they really cared about how they looked. I love the irony of the fact that by putting a suit on, they became gentlemen. Brilliant.

Exhibit B:

The Bloods and Crips of LA. It's not 'gangster' anymore with this lot – its gangsta. These are the new school, if you like – you saw them in *Boyz'n' the Hood* and *Colors* and realised gang-bangin'* had another meaning. *Straight Outta Compton* by NWA grabbed you by the bollocks and you bought 2001 by Dr Dre; you quite fancied one of those huge cars with the bouncy suspension. You even tried drinking Hennessy Cognac because Dre and Xzibit rap about it.

It's another concept that drifted over from America – the likes of Dre and Snoop came from these gangs before making it big, rapped about life on the streets and shooting people, and Gangsta Rap was born. It's a very negative image – we see it in the news all the time, with words such as guns, drugs and violence following closely behind. Take a walk down through Dalston, or Peckham, or the back streets of Birmingham, Manchester or Bristol and you'll see Garage scene kids walking round . . . when they're not shooting people up with their reactivated Mac-10s. For the mainstream, there's been stuff like *Lock, Stock and Two Smoking Barrels*, *Snatch* and, in 2006, *Rollin' with the Nines*, one of the least PC and most violent movies made in the past 20 years. It's a great film, I think, but then I'm biased: I played one of the lead roles. More on that later.

None of these films promote a gangster lifestyle: it all looks great at the start, but there's always a downfall, always a moral message.

I've seen and mixed with nearly every type of gangster you'd care to mention. I've been labelled as one by people who don't even know me. In the work I've done over the years, I've had to have a team with me – this is probably where all the misconceptions started from and they've followed me around ever since. It's a curse. Being young and successful with a nice car and nice house meant that I was either a gangster and up to no good, or a drug dealer. There is no middle ground, it seems.

When you're walking around knocking on doors with a bunch of big, tasty-looking, flat-nosed geezers, people are going to put two and two together though, aren't they? They will always think you're up to no good, regardless of what you are doing. And it's not like we were knocking on doors to sell Bibles. So maybe they had a point. In a way.

I did a bit of debt collecting, which is a job that usually requires more than one person. It was only a few years ago when debt collecting was about intimidation – these days collectors are civilised and have a chat with their 'clients'. The world's gone mad. One of my mates makes a lot of money as a debt collector. He's civilised and polite, but will still turn nasty if anyone takes the piss. He was recovering some money from a geezer not too long ago – he owed a substantial stash and when my mate met him to pick it up, the geezer came out with, 'What will you do if I decide not to pay you?'

This was puzzling. They'd already talked it over a few times and this meeting was to pay the debt and that be the end of it.

'Are you telling me you're not going to pay?' he asked.

'Why? Will you knock me out if I don't pay?' asked the geezer.

My mate was losing his temper, 'Are you going to pay me the money or not?'

'No'.

Bang. One punch and the guy was sparko. My mate took the money from his pocket as he lay there. It was already in an envelope. What was he thinking?

For me, debt collecting was just an extension of door work because people knew I was handy when it came to sorting trouble out. I'd get calls asking if I'd pick up money that was owed to people and I did alright by it.

There was a club in Camberley called Agincourt where me and my mate Joe Johnson used to run the security. I was in my early 20s, aggressive, up for anything . . . Joe was as mad as a sack of monkeys and when people were owed money and had no way of getting it, they'd ask us to do it because we didn't give a fuck. The combination of being young with a reputation to uphold and enhance and the responsibility of having to get results was pretty dangerous.

There's a fine line between collecting a debt and terrorising some poor fucker – if they told me they would not or could not pay up, the usual approach was to threaten them for payment on the next visit. If they still couldn't or wouldn't pay, I'd have to carry that threat out. If I phoned someone and told them to pay up, I'd tell them who I was and to look me up if they needed to, then to call me back and tell me if they were going to pay or not. They wouldn't get lippy once they knew who I was and who was with me.

If they were expecting a punch in the mouth, it may just be worth taking the chance of non-payment, but if they thought they'd be driven somewhere and have holes drilled into their kneecaps, they'd pay up. No problem.

In that scenario, the threat of violence is far worse than the actual violence itself. It was all about conning people, really. Debts were usually around ten grand and I'd get offered 30% to collect it. But that was just loose change compared to what I started earning from raves, so I was wasting my time doing it. And to be honest, I didn't want to get involved with other people's problems, which is what debt collecting is. You have to be a full time people-hater, and I'm quite the opposite. Terrorism and aggravation are two things I don't like – I'd gone from playing the part of a thug to being one. If I didn't watch out, I'd end up being a gangster.

There's a load of people out there who'd love to be thought of that way. I'm the opposite. If I'd wanted to be a gangster, I could have been one. My CV had all the right qualifications and I know enough of them to sign up if I was that way inclined. Not for me. I've seen loads of right old mugs – not only in music – trying to be Johnny Big Bananas, walking the walk and unable to talk the talk. It's a pretty sad sight.

My initiation to the London underworld came after Ronnie Kray's funeral in 1995.

All the papers covered the funeral, and they were full of one name: Dave Courtney.

Described as a top London Gangster in all media reports, he certainly looked the part, surrounded by a load of heavies and taking care of security for this huge East End event. Dave was overseeing everything, in his element. It made his name, and he became the new face of British crime. Dave wasn't exactly media-shy – to say the least – and documentaries and magazine articles followed as he introduced himself to a new audience and quickly became a marketable brand. No one had heard of British gangsters since the Krays and this geezer was an associate of theirs, quick-witted and with the personality of a criminal-come-entertainer. He took the Krays' invention of a celebrity criminal that step further – to baldly go where no other gangster had gone before.

We decided we'd interview his bird, Jenny, for *The Scene*, which was still going at the time. She was trying to make a name for herself as a rapper and with Dave attracting so much publicity she could use it to her advantage. I went along – I was interested in meeting Dave, as I'd always been fascinated by the Krays – and we got talking. He asked me what I did for a living and his eyes lit up when I told him about the raves. To say he was interested would be an understatement – he was itching to get into the scene as much as he could.

We got on well – we came from similar backgrounds, knew a lot of the same people and, both being on the club scene in our owns ways, we shared some of the same interests. I also knew he'd boxed in the past and was quite fond of a row . . . what else would you look for in a new acquaintance?

As our friendship progressed, he started writing for the magazine. We gave him a regular column called Dodgy Dave's Funny Page, where he just wrote any old bollocks. (You're starting to get a feel for our regular features.) It gave him a platform to mouth off about anything, adding his own unique style and allowing his personality to shine through. People looked forward to their Dodgy columnist's rantings and would always fast forward to the back pages to see what he'd been up to each month. There were a few editions where we changed the title to Dodgy Dave Live From The Inside when he'd been locked up in HMP Belmarsh for something or other. I've still got copies of the magazine and was looking through them recently – reading Dave's pages, you'd think he was an absolute nutcase: *Well, there's only a few more money-spunking days till fucking Christmas. I've stolen the kids some nice presents this year. I hit the old cheque book and card well hard, and whoever the poor bastard is that owns it now owes the bank a good few quid. I even sent a fat moody cheque to the police widows' Christmas fund for a laugh.*

He came along to a few raves, arriving with all his boys – a fucking huge posse of them. Looking back, it was funny. He really knows how to make an entrance. A lot of people in the club knew who he was through the funeral thing alone, and being the most conspicuous person you're ever likely to come across, no one could miss that Dave was in the house. Dave met my Team, of course: he could see immediately that I had respect and that my firm wouldn't be with me if I was just some idiot. It definitely was a show of strength and I could see Dave's mind start ticking over, thinking, *Fuck me – where did he find this lot?*

Neither of us being stupid, we worked out that we could use each other to our mutual advantage. We got chatting seriously one night and came to an agreement. I could use his name and growing reputation as back up – if people knew I was mates with him, it would sort out and stop a lot of the potential trouble that was never far away, with jealous rivals, dickheads trying it on for protection and drug dealers trying to muscle in. We could cope with them ourselves, but being connected to Courtney might mean we never even had to: he had some scary geezers onside, and having him vouch for us would help keep the shit away. It made me more of a face in London, where I'd always been conscious that I was an outsider from sleepy little Camberley.

From Dave's point of view, he could come along to the raves, have a good time, be noticed and build his reputation.

We shook hands and had a drink on it.

Dave was my first real contact within the gangster fraternity. He proved to be a valuable person to know, most of the time. I was invited to all the parties and the boxing dos, meeting all the villains – top people like Wilf Pine, Roy Shaw, Freddie Foreman, Tony Lambrianou, Bruce Reynolds, Charlie Richardson, the Nashes, Frank Fraser and Joey Pyle. I never did any business with them, but they were interesting guys, all time-served in their trades and well-respected in the Underworld, and now retired and enjoying the world of the Celebrity Gangster. I liked meeting them – they were my type of people and, of course, it suited me and my career at the time to know them. I'd sit and watch the 'civvies' at these events coming up, wanting to buy them drinks and have their photo taken with them. It was great for networking and, as with Dave, we had a lot in common. OK, I wasn't a criminal mastermind or a convicted murderer, but my world, of door security, the club scene and debt collecting shares common threads with the world of organised crime. I spent night after night swapping stories and getting along famously with the cream of crime, and it all helped build my network up. I know it sounds like a contradiction, but they were a decent bunch – they'd been around in the '50s and '60s and had a sense of honour about their business that's long gone now. Most 'gangsters' today are generally just wannabe cunts with guns, crack-heads in hoodies; they don't compare to the romantic vision of the boys in the 60s.

Of course, they were every bit as likely to shoot you in the face or cut your stomach open, but they'd have done it with style and with a nice suit on.

One of the old school guys I got to know I stayed really close to, because he really impressed me, and that was my mate Wilf Pine. Wilf is intelligent, he's a proper gentleman and he doesn't bullshit you. He's a genuine bloke and is respected the world over because of it. I think he's still the only Englishman reputed to be a made man in the Mafia (according to US Law Enforcement agencies). When I met him, it was over a situation where someone was accused of being a rat and he wanted to see me. We sat down and discussed it and everything was smoothed out. From that day, we became friends. I still see him regularly – and have done over 10 years now. He's been able to vouch for me on more than one occasion and is the only person I know of who can arrange anything for you anywhere on the planet. Unlike the rest of the gangster fraternity, Wilf hasn't got a criminal record and has never done time, so he's as clean as a whistle. As our friendship grew, Wilf became a kind of father figure to me and I'm honoured that he calls me the son he never had, phoning me up and going, 'Terry, it's your Jewish father calling.' That doesn't happen with anyone else. He really is the nicest bloke you could ever meet – but you wouldn't want to upset him.

I said to him once, 'I wish I'd met you when I was 16 or 17, you know.'

He replied with, 'No you fucking well don't,' and we laughed for too long. He was probably right; fuck knows what kind of trouble we'd have got ourselves into.

Some of the American guys I've met through Wilf are pretty heavy-duty. I've been to the best restaurants and clubs with them and each time we'd get the best table, best service and the chef coming out to see us. It really is a *Goodfellas* world. One time, when I was over in Vegas with Jez Bailey, Wilf set me up with some friends of his and they really made sure we got the VIP treatment. There was a restaurant where all the stars went and you had to book up months in advance to eat there. If you know the right people though, you could just stroll in and get the best table in the house. And that's exactly what we did.

'Follow me please, Mr Turbo. We have been expecting you.'

We sat down and were having a look round, sussing the menu out, when the waiter came along with a telephone, 'It's for you Mr Turbo, sir.'

It was our American mates. I thanked him for getting us in and he said it was their pleasure to help us out, then said to make sure we took care of the waiter.

'Hang on. You want me to take care of the waiter?' I asked.

'Yeah, man. Take care of the guy,' he said.

'What? Like, *take care* of him? Are you sure?'

There was a few seconds silence then roaring laughter, 'Terry, you fucking crazy maniac. *Tip* the guy. Don't fucking bury him in the desert!' he said.

Of course the waiter was listening and gave us the best service he'd ever given in his life. It was an amazing night on an amazing holiday, courtesy of a more than amazing friend.

It's great that people say they'll back you up and even better when they actually do it. I'd just taken a new place on a while back – nice classy restaurant, new venture and keen to make it happen. We'd not been in business that long when some geezers came in one day and started taking photos inside and out, making the staff feel very nervous. The manager asked why and they said they were lost. Were they for real? He moved them on and made a note of their car. It was quite a rare top of the range motor so I knew it wouldn't be too hard to find some info on the owners.

I made a few calls and found out they were armed robbers and were obviously out on a reconnaissance mission to do my place over. I phoned Wilf and he soon traced them through friends of ours. As luck would have it, someone paid those two would-be robbers a visit and it was made clear that they should wipe my property off their list and never step foot in there again. Funnily enough I haven't seen them since. That was it – problem sorted with a few phone calls – a result from using the old boys' network. With things like that, I could ask Wilf for any favour and he would help me out. He'd do anything for a mate, he gives me advice on a weekly basis and he's never once asked for anything in return. It isn't a favour for favour deal with him – he's a straight-up guy and someone I'm proud to call a friend.

Meanwhile, Dave Courtney and I had some real laughs together. In '97, We held our biggest Garage Nation party at the G-Mex in Manchester, in partnership with Fantazia. There were 15,000 there and it was one of the best nights ever. Fantazia did most of the organisation so me and the boys were able to go up there and enjoy ourselves. We hired a minibus, and took Dave along. We checked into this five star hotel, where all the DJs were staying – the likes of Carl Cox, Paul Oakenfold and Sasha – with loads of models and other celebs. Dave called us into his room half an hour after we checked in. He had a holdall on the bed.

'Right, boys,' he said. 'You know what these northern cunts are like up here for guns and shit? There's no fucking way we're going anywhere here without the proper tools.'

He opened the bag and dumped the contents on his bed. Uzis, Mac-10s, .357 Magnums, 9mm automatics… the fucking works. Everyone's eyes popped out and he started cackling. They were imitations. He insisted on taking a Mac-10 to the party for a piss-take. Obviously, it set the metal detector off.

Doorman, doing a double take: 'Er . . . you can't bring that in here.'

Dave: 'What you on about? I ain't going in there without it.'

Doorman: 'Er . . . sorry but . . .'

Dave: 'Relax . . . I'm having a laugh you cunt.'

We pissed ourselves.

Back at the hotel, we're sitting in the lobby and the lift comes down. The doors open and this huge fuck-off display firework starts firing rockets into the lobby, with everyone diving for cover. Courtney again: you could almost hear the bastard cackling.

So, we got on well. But we were never really close mates or anything and, after a while, we sort of drifted apart. I'd stopped going to the gangster parties and I'd not seen Dave for months. He was great company, but he brought a lot of baggage and aggravation with him, probably without meaning to.

Imagine my surprise, then, when I started hearing on the grapevine a year or so later that I had another partner, called D. Courtney, Esq. Apparently, he was going round telling everyone who would listen that he was running my raves, which was more than I'd bargained for when we'd agreed to use each others' names for mutual benefit.

Fuck me, I'd learned that lesson with Letraset Mark and his mate Andy, and Phil and Mick, the Tottenham geezers who I did The Rocket with. Apart from Jason Kaye, the one thing I didn't want, or need, was another partner – especially one who was so fucking secret even I didn't know about it.

Worse still, he brought out a book – *Raving Lunacy* – in which he continued claiming he was my business partner. You may be wondering why I was bothered. Well, Dave, being the type of person he is, had sent copies to a lot of top people – including the then Metropolitan Police Commissioner Sir Paul Condon, the VAT man, the tax man and the Queen, for fuck's sake. I'm sure he thought that was hilarious, and I'd have seen the funny side myself if it had been about anyone else.

Even fucking worse, he'd made up a load of other stuff about me in the book. He'd asked me if I minded him mentioning a few things about me in it, and the stories he suggested were fine. They were a lot fucking different in print, sadly.

There I am, named and shamed in the pages, as having been in a car with Dave in a crazed gun battle, like something from *Starsky and Hutch*.

That was serious shit. For a start – and for the record – it was bollocks. I never was in any car with anyone in any kind of gun battle. I was a businessman, earning a good living by being the face of a successful organisation; I was not Ned fucking Kelly.

Why on earth would I be driving around with Dave, getting shot at? More important than it being untrue, it was accusing me of having committed a serious criminal offence and I did not want the Old Bill nosing around me any more than anyone else does. They might even think it had the ring of truth – I had a 9mm pistol, perfectly legit, and the cops knew that because they were involved in the licensing process.

I had a right go at Dave but he laughed it off, which disappointed me.

Even so, I could have laughed it off myself, eventually, if it hadn't caused me genuine grief.

You could almost hear the Tax Man and the VAT Man chatting in their local boozer.

Have you read this book that Dave Courtney's sent us?

Dave who?

Dave Courtney . . . the notorious hard-core criminal and gangster.

No . . . what's it say?

It says some geezer called Terry Turbo's his business partner.

Well, if Turbo's his partner, he must be a hard core criminal and gangster, too.

Do hard core criminals and gangsters pay their taxes and VAT bills?

Do they fuck!

Let's have a close look at Mr T Turbo. In fact, let's spin the cunt.

They launched a full-scale investigation into me and my businesses. It's the oldest trick in the book – tax dodging brought Capone down, after all.

I thanked the Lord I'd taken the decision to go proper legit. Everything I'd ever earned was scrutinised, they turned my house over and all my paperwork and accounts. Raves were a cash business and they were crawling all over me, looking for the tiniest mistake or something that didn't quite balance up correctly.

At first, I just thought I'd been unlucky to get a pull, and didn't put two and two together. But they kept asking me if I had a business partner.

'No.'

'Are you sure?'

'Yes.'

'Really sure?'

'Utterly, totally, fucking, completely, 100 per cent sure.'

'Really?'

'Yes, really. Why d'you keep banging on about it?'

'Have you read the book?'

'Have I read what book?'

'Dave Courtney's book. He says you're his partner in it.'

With a friend like that, who the fuck needs any enemies?

My accountant, Frances was a diamond. First, she squared the Customs and Excise and Inland Revenue away. I'd been straight, between us we proved it and that was that. Then she set me even straighter on how things were going to be from here on in.

'Even though you and I know you're honest,' she said, 'they don't believe it. They're going to be on your case from now on. They'll look at every penny you've ever handled, they'll be outside your events clicking everyone in on the doors, they'll be in the record shops finding out how many tickets had been sold and in the clubs to get how much was taken over the bar to work out numbers. They'll investigate anyone you do business with, they'll turn over DJs, tap your phone, be all over your bank accounts and follow you everywhere.'

Fuck me. I might as well change my name to Terry Capone.

Everyone who's in business takes a bit of cash, and if they say they don't they're either stupid or liars. Now there was a third category: me. If I wasn't careful, I could get fucked and lose everything.

'If you take £30,000 on a night,' said Frances, 'you can't even take £50 for your petrol money home unless you put it through the books.'

I tried to understand Dave's motives. Maybe in his own way, he was trying to big me up and earn me a reputation as a face – I don't know. But whatever – I didn't want the reputation or the heat that goes with being a face. If he had asked, 'Do you mind if I make a story up about us driving along and having a shoot-out?' I'd have asked him what the fuck he was on. Even if it was true, it's hardly something I'd want people knowing about.

Don't get me wrong – Dave's a solid geezer and he certainly can have a row, I'm not disputing that. He was into debt collecting and had a lot of respect. Even after all of this, I'm still friends with him; we're not as close as we used to be, but he's helped me out in a lot of situations, has collected money for me and made some phone calls for me. He's gone above and beyond the call of duty for me and proved that he was a mate in many ways. Dave is a likeable geezer and a great laugh: he'll drop you in the shit and offer you a drink in the next breath.

The whole fucking gangster thing caused me a lot of grief. I can laugh about it now because – outside a few proper people – it's all bullshit. Some of the supposed 'gangster' stuff that goes on was and still is hilarious. There's internet forums now where all these people take sides and argue with each other about who is the top gangster, who is a grass, who isn't a real gangster, who is the hardest, who is an informant – it's mental. Rumours, Chinese Whispers and lies have always kept people fighting; the internet has just provided a quicker and bigger way to spread it around. There are enough gangster stories that have been circulating for years – people have even been interviewed on TV about them and told porkies to better their own reputation. With so much bollocks and falseness, its little wonder that people see that lifestyle as full of petty squabbling, back-stabbing and fucking wannabes telling lies and bullshitting everyone.

Speaking of which.

I know this sounds like the opening line to a terrible joke, but bear with me. There was this African prince called something unpronounceable.

He was also known as Iks, he ran an organisation called Dance Planet and he seemed alright. Put it this way, of all the African princes I knew, he was the one I got on with the best. I took him at face-value. He had a few bad habits – well, he was a fucking cokehead – but everyone's entitled to their vices, and being a dodgy geezer can always be a rumour.

How wrong can you be?

He turned out to be a right fucking wanker.

I'd been friendly with him for years. We weren't mates, but we knocked around together in the same small sliver of society and he was usually good for a laugh.

Then he placed an advert in *The Scene* for one of his events and conveniently forgot to pay the invoice.

After three or four months, I started phoning him and sending repeat invoices. It wasn't a lot of dough – in fact, it was the princely sum of three hundred quid. But it was the principle that mattered. I was pretty disgusted. It wasn't the kind of shit that I expected, to be honest. We were in the same business and you don't do that to people you know (or anyone else, in my book).

I started asking around and found out that he wasn't just a dodgy fucker, he was also a two-faced, dishonest, debt-ridden bag of shit. Well at least I'd found out what he was like before he owed me a lot of money.

He was dodging my calls and ignoring my letters until he finally answered his phone one day. I couldn't hold back. 'Iks,' I said. 'Where's my fucking money, you fucking cunt?' As opening lines go, it wasn't bad. He was lucky we weren't talking face to face. I'd had plenty of time stewing and I'd probably have taken his head off.

Amazingly, he tried to brazen it out. He wasn't going to pay, he said, and what was I going to do about it?

I told him that the next time we met there would be a serious punch-up and I would fucking destroy him.

It didn't make any difference, he still wasn't paying.

I put the phone down, mystified. I couldn't believe that he was willing to risk getting a proper kicking off me for the sake of three hundred quid. Maybe he thought I was bluffing. Maybe he was right. I might have given him a slap if I'd run into him a day or two later but would I really have kicked him all around the floor for a few poxy quid? I may go a bit daft at times but I certainly wasn't stupid and I wouldn't risk going to prison for him. My aim was really to put the fear of God into him. He'd never set foot anywhere he thought I'd be and if I went to one of his shitty events he'd have to spend the night hiding. It was a nice bit of mental torture for him – as satisfying as having him bumped off, in a sick kind of way. For the next few days, I'd rant on to anyone who'd listen that I wanted to do Iks in, thinking that if more people knew about it, then the chances were that it would get back to him and put the shits up him even more.

I gave him one last chance to pay before putting it to rest. I phoned him again to see if no was still his final answer, after having had a while to think it over. He didn't pick up so I had to assume his original reply still stood. I didn't want to waste any more money by running my phone bill up as well.

And there the story ought to have ended. Instead, next day the CID hammered my front door in while I was asleep.

Two of them burst in and, without so much as a, 'Good morning, Terry', one of them showed me a search warrant.

'You're being arrested for aggravated burglary and GBH with intent,' he said.

Fuck me. Those were serious charges, with jail time attached, and that did stop me in my tracks a bit. *Aggravated burglary? GBH with intent?* Like all of us, my memory was getting worse as I got older but this was news to me.

'I think you've got the wrong man, officers,' I said.

But they ignored me and started turning my house over. I watched, feeling pretty bloody amazed. I wondered if *CrimeWatch* had just been on and I looked like some geezer on it? I was mystified.

'Look, can I help you at all?' I said, as I watched them rooting through my cupboards. 'If you tell me what you're looking for I might be able to assist you?'

'We're searching for knuckle dusters and bloodstained clothing,' said one of them.

'Ah,' I said. 'In that case, I don't think I can help you, after all. You won't find either of those things here, honestly. I really think you must have the wrong man.'

I'm the kind of person who tends to make light of difficult situations. Sometimes, I fuck myself up with bad taste jokes intended to lighten the mood. This was one of those times. I reached for my dummy knife and shouted, 'You'll never take me alive, coppers!' and 'stabbed' one of them.

He looked at me like I was some sort of twat, and it didn't lighten the mood at all. Far from it. Looking back, that was no surprise. I'm not a dangerous, knife-wielding mentalist but how were they expected to know that? I'm lucky they weren't armed. I probably would have been shot dead in my own bedroom.

After ransacking the entire house, they didn't find any knuckle dusters or bloodstained clothing, as predicted by yours truly – but they didn't want to be reminded of that so I kept schtum.

They were intrigued when they discovered my safe, however. OK, a safe is a bit unusual but they're not *that* uncommon. I brought tens of thousands of pounds home with me on weekends, and it wouldn't fit under the mattress. And you should have seen their faces when I opened it up for them to take a butcher's inside. They started drooling. They'd hit the jackpot! There before them was a Browning 9mm handgun with two hundred rounds of ammunition. OK, again, a gun is fairly unusual. But this was in the days before handguns were illegal and, as I've said, I held it perfectly legitimately. I had a licence for it and went shooting regularly. It was no big deal to me, just a pastime that I enjoyed. To these two, it was like they'd caught Bernardo Provenzano.

Naturally, I made a joke out of it. I mean, someone had to break the silence.

'Ah,' I said. 'The tools of the trade. I'm a professional hitman you see. Not a great job, in some ways, but it pays well.'

When *will* I learn?

They were a tough crowd, these boys. The only thing missing was tumbleweed blowing past.

Terry's Tip Of The Day: If your house is raided early doors by the police, *do not* pretend to attack them with a toy knife and *do not* joke about being a hit man when they find your gun and ammo in your safe. It just isn't worth it.

I showed them my licence and, unsurprisingly, they showed me to their car. They didn't cuff me – I think they'd realised I wasn't likely to get violent or resist arrest, though they were probably wary of custard pies – but they did drive me to Woking nick. I waited there for nearly five hours before they carted me off up to Oxford nick. I wasn't laughing any more. I was beginning to realise that this was no ordinary arrest, though they wouldn't give me any details. Something wasn't right and I had a bad feeling inside.

At Oxford, they arranged a duty brief and filled me in. (Not like they used to in the good old days, I mean they informed me as to what was going on).

A Detective Inspector came into the interview room and sat down opposite us.

'It's like this,' he said. 'First off, due to the seriousness of the charge and our concerns about your behaviour, we are impounding your pistol and ammunition. Your licence is being revoked.'

'OK,' I said. I could argue about the gun later. 'What *is* this all about?'

He started talking about Iks and my brain went into overload. *Fucking Iks!*

'. . . and he was badly beaten in his own house.'

Great, I thought, *couldn't have happened to a nicer bloke.*

'But why have I been arrested?' I said.

'The Injured Party has named you as being in a group of four men who carried out the assault.'

Fuck me, the cunt.

Apparently, a few weeks earlier, Dave Courtney, two unnamed heavies and I had driven to Oxford in a white diesel saloon car looking for Iks. Once we found his house (for the record, I had never been to his house and he never gave his address out, so how would I fucking know where he lived?), we'd kicked his door in in broad daylight and beat a new shade of shit out of him. Allegedly, we were all wearing knuckle dusters at the time, hence the early morning search of my gaff.

'You're joking,' I said. Which was a bit of a role reversal from earlier.

But they were deadly serious. And it certainly didn't feel very funny being in my shoes.

'Look,' I said. 'You really have got the wrong man here. I haven't been anywhere near Oxford, with Dave Courtney or anyone else. I don't know what Iks' game is but he's taking the piss. He owed me three hundred poxy quid. Yes, I was pissed off. I'm sure you would be, too. But think about it . . . driving to Oxford, taking three other guys with me, expenses, petrol money . . . even if I'd wanted to do it, which I didn't, it would have cost me loads more than I was owed.'

They looked at me, blankly.

'And why would I take three other guys with me?' I said. 'I've collected debts for a living and I wouldn't have much trouble with Iks. I wouldn't have needed them, it's absurd and slightly insulting. Anyway, if four blokes *had* teamed up on him using dusters, he'd be dead or close to it, not talking to you lot. It just doesn't add up.'

They didn't seem that impressed with all that, though. They kept asking questions.

'What about the white diesel saloon car identified by the Injured Party?' said one of them. 'You've got one of those. A Seat Toledo.'

It was true I did have a battered old diesel Toledo. It was a second car, one that I used as a run-around because it cost fuck

The legend that is Jason Kaye, with some guy with silly hair. Below, my mate Murray Beetson takes the helm as we enjoy the sun in St Lucia. Unbelievably, a week later he was dead.

On the beers with Slipmatt in Ibiza. Check out the bling. And Goldie and me mess around at Brixton Academy during my last One Nation. Max looks like a burden's lifted from her shoulders - probably because I won't be spending my nights punching crackheads with guns any more.

Puff Daddy - P Diddy as he now is - with me and my mate Owen Gardner in
Ibiza. We're just about to go on the piss with him! Below, me and Adam Saint
try to decide between burgers and kebabs in Ayia Napa. Megaman and Romeo
from the So Solid Crew are healthy eaters, so they'll just be having the salad.

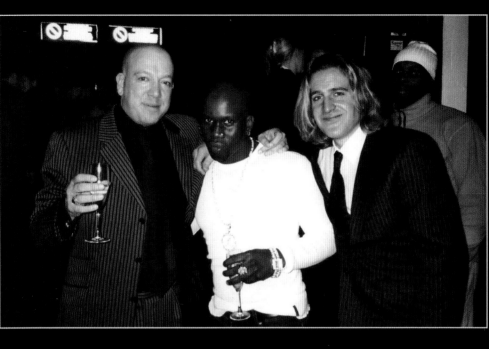

Enjoying a glass of shampoo with Mark Morrison and Julian Gilbey, who directed me in Rollin' With The Nines. Below, ringside in Vegas for a Lennox Lewis fight, with pal James Hewitt.

Jimmy Kent, Billy Murray and Dave Courtney with me on the set of Dave's film Hell To Pay. Billy and me are now business partners. Below, a production still from One Man And His Dog, with the great Bobby George and BBC sports journalist Ray Stubbs.

The really important things in life. With my daughter Jade and my baby boy, Alfie. I'm determined to be the best dad I can be.

all to run and I could do all my picking up and dropping off in it without my proper motor getting keyed and doing a million miles. I knew I hadn't been up to Oxford in it on the day in question, but it did worry me a bit. Some of the boys used it from time to time, too. Maybe one of them had heard me ranting and gone up there to find Iks and do him for me? Thinking he'd get the money and do me a massive favour? I hoped to fuck they hadn't.

'What about this car, then?' asked the copper.

Unsure, I declined to comment. I didn't want to say anything that could drop me or anyone else in the shit.

'Where were you on the day in question?'

'No comment,' I said. I was fairly sure I'd been in a meeting with a good friend of mine, Stuart Reid, who ran the Eclipse rave club in Coventry. Stuart had previous firearms offences and had served time for them. If I named him, and they did their poking around, it would look like a dodgy meeting between two criminal masterminds. They always assume the worst, and I didn't want to fuel the fire. Added to that, I have such a shit memory it was possible I was wrong. If I had to change my story later it would look like I was lying to cover something up. Better to make sure Stuart recalled the meet, warn him I'd be naming him and do it later.

The questions kept coming and I kept batting them back. I knew I had nothing to hide and I was sure this was a simple case of mistaken identity that would eventually be sorted out. There was no doubt *someone* had given Iks a good kicking, and it wasn't really that surprising. He was the type who made enemies. He'd upset someone and they'd fucked him up – and if I'd have found out who I'd have bought them a pint. All *I* knew was it wasn't me, whatever the silly sod was saying. Maybe he wanted revenge for my phone threats, and a bit of compensation along the way? The question was, could I convince the police of this?

There was a break in proceedings and I had a quick chat with the duty solicitor. I was still fairly confident this would all be sorted out. But you have to ask the question, don't you?

'What's the worst I can expect?' I asked.

'Well, if convicted you're looking at a minimum of five years,' he said.

Five fucking years! That was a reality check. My heart sank. I closed my eyes and let the words wash over me. It was a fucking nightmare. When you see films where this happens, you think, *Just tell them you didn't do it and they'll believe you.* You can't imagine it ever happening, and for most people, it won't. Now it was happening to me. No one would listen. I was Richard Kimble in *The Fugitive.*

I was released on bail and told where the taxi rank was. I hope the police are better-mannered these days, fucking hell.

I made a few phone calls when I eventually got home.

There were a few lines of enquiry of my own I could pursue.

First, the car.

Here, I got lucky. Frances Williams, my accountant, got her diary out. Turns out she'd had her car in the garage on the day the beating had happened. This was before courtesy cars were invented – you had to fend for yourself, or borrow one from a mate for a couple of days, so she'd phoned one of the boys, borrowed the Toledo and solved her temporary transport problem. Frances was a respectable professional woman, not a rave promoter with hordes of dodgy mates. That gave the vehicle an alibi, for starters.

What about one for me?

I checked my own diary. Yep, I'd been meeting Stuart Reid about tape pack distribution. I called Stuart up to check he could confirm everything. It sounds mad to ask someone you just had a meeting with if you actually *did* have a meeting, but the entire case was off its head in the first place. Stuart was willing to be a witness to prove that I couldn't have been in Oxford and I thanked him, putting the phone down with an amazing sense of relief.

My next call was to the police.

I told them about the car, where I was and who I was with and apologised for not answering their questions on the day.

'This proves the whole thing is rubbish, surely?' I said. 'I was in a different part of the country and the car Iks says we were in was being used by a respectable professional person. That must be reason enough to drop the case?'

No chance. It was all in the legal system by then. A very fucking slow legal system. At least the copper told me that he'd made a note of the phone conversation and it would go into my file for reference. Great. Thanks for your help, officer.

It took nine months for the case to come to trial, nine months of anguish, wondering what the outcome would be. And women complain about nine months of pregnancy.

During that time, the CID paid Stuart a visit. Apparently, they advised him that, because of his record, no one would believe him in court and not to bother turning up or they would nick him for perjury. Charming.

Naturally, he told them to fuck off.

They also visited Frances to make sure that her story was correct. It was.

Naturally, she asked them to leave.

I was unable to apply for legal aid because I have always earned money and paid my taxes. This meant that I'd have to pay for my own legal representation, forking out for a barrister and solicitor to defend me. The estimated cost for all this came to five grand. Iks was starting to cost me a lot of money and it made me determined that he wouldn't cost me my freedom. If I was found guilty, I was looking at five years of bird or more. Years of my life could be wasted because an African prince placed an advert in my magazine and refused to pay the three hundred quid charge – all I did was phone him up a few times to get my money and swear at him a lot.

My barrister was Jayne Terry. After our first meeting, she painted a pretty serious picture.

'To be honest, Terry,' she said, 'the fact that you didn't tell the police on interview where your car was or where you were on the day in question will go against you in court. But even with the alibis you've only got a 50/50 chance of winning because it will just come down to who the jury believes. If they believe you, you walk. If they believe Iks, you go to jail.'

It was a major downer, though there was no point Jayne bullshitting me. It felt like the odds were massively stacked against me. I was torturing myself every fucking day wondering how I ended up in this shit.

I've seen dozens of people go to prison for so many reasons, mainly silly ones. I can't think of many things worth losing your freedom for. I've heard people say they'll happily go to jail for beating someone up, for instance. Why? What's the attraction? I don't understand it. If someone owes you 300 quid, is it worth beating the fuck out of him and going to prison for five years? Let's say on a five-year stretch, you do three on good behaviour. That makes your freedom worth a hundred quid a year. Not very much when you think of it like that . . . less than two quid a week, in fact. If you've got no home, no family and no life, then prison doesn't seem too bad. Maybe it's a masculine thing to sound like you'd be willing to be sent down on the principle that you clumped someone for doing wrong, I don't know. I've cringed when mates of mine have had a laugh and a joke in court, thinking it would get them off. They've said things like, 'Yeah, I broke his jaw. But he's a cunt.'

You can make a jury laugh, you can (try to) make a judge laugh, but in the end they'll still lock you up. They don't let you off for being funny and they don't send you to a special clown prison for funny criminals, either.

The whole experience, the waiting game, took me right to the edge of sanity. I had to drag myself round each morning, make a real effort to function, and take every kind of potion I could find to help boost my energy levels. It didn't work because my brain felt alert but my body wasn't interested – an active mind, passive body, and lack of motivation are not a good combination. My sleep pattern was all over the place and I was on an endless cycle of misery.

The closer we got to the trial, the worse I felt. The more drained I felt, the more I convinced myself that the worst would happen.

Before, I'd been the most optimistic person around. Now, I was totally deflated and couldn't see a bright side to anything. Imagine you're sinking in quicksand and struggling to hang on to a branch to save yourself. I was sinking, but couldn't be bothered reaching out for branches.

The only way out I could see was to commit suicide. Really. I could have ended it all just by doing that one thing; there was no point in kidding myself that everything would work out fine. A few pills, some Scotch . . . I'd be released.

At my next legal meeting, I was told to grow my hair, get some reading glasses and buy myself a light grey coloured suit. When I asked why, the answer was, 'Because you look like trouble, and first impressions count.'

Fair enough. Jayne was the expert and I was more than willing to take any advice to increase my chances. A six-foot, well-built skinhead carries all the connotations of a thug – no two ways about it. Within a few months I had transformed myself into a right geek: part teacher, part civil servant, I felt sure I'd got the image right because most of my mates didn't even recognise me in the street. It was only after this meeting that I decided not to give up and take the easy way out. Any cunt in the world can top themselves when they hit a rough patch. There's nothing difficult about it; it will all be over and there will be nothing to worry about ever again. The downside is you'd be fucking dead, and I didn't want to be dead yet.

I'm no quitter. I never have been and I never will be. I made arrangements for my mum to take control. I detailed everything, from A to Z – how to run this and that, how procedures worked, who to deal with, who to see if there were any problems – she could probably have managed to keep it all ticking over, but I knew that without me there to keep an eye on the business, there would be plenty of vultures waiting to swoop. My mum, bless her, was willing to take them all on single-handedly. She would have done anything to help. I bet she'd have gone round and topped Iks to get me out of the mess.

As the case approached, I moved from fatalism to slight optimism. I had to show determination and fight for what was mine. If being innocent until being proved guilty really existed, I had to play it cool. He was the one who had to do all the work. I started to feel like I had a fighting chance of winning.

A phone call from Iks a few days before the case confirmed it.

He told me that if I gave him ten grand, he wouldn't turn up for the trial and I'd get off. I knew in that instant that he didn't fancy his chances of winning.

'Listen you piece of shit,' I said. 'I'd rather pay someone £10,000 to kill you and bury you. Don't ever phone me again. I'll see you in court.'

February 1998: Non-Paying Cunt vs Turbo, at Oxford Crown Court. I was nervous, but psyched. I sat at the back of the room and listened to the prosecution outline the case to the judge, without the jury present. He really fucking went for it, launching into a lecture about organised crime, the Krays and Dave Courtney, and how I was also an organised criminal.

Dave's fucking book, again. When will this fucking end?

This lawyer even fucking convinced me: even if I had the Pope as a character witness, no one would believe me after that. I *knew* I was going to jail.

The judge, thank fuck, uses this part of the trial to say whether the speeches are alright or need to be changed. Jayne knew what she was doing. She objected to the opening statement. 'It's Mr Turbo who is on trial today, Your Honour,' she said. 'Not the Krays or Dave Courtney. Mr Turbo has never even met the Krays.' These were names that scare people and by associating me with them the prosecution was tying me in to their way of behaving.

We managed to get the charges reduced, too – a doctor who did a lot of work with the Metropolitan Police said the injuries Iks had sustained were not concurrent with four geezers wearing knuckle dusters punching the fuck out of him. As a result of this, the judge dropped my charge from aggravated burglary with all the trimmings down to ABH. That still carried a maximum sentence of five years, and Jayne warned me that the judge would issue the full five, given the circumstances, if I was found guilty.

I tried not to take this with negativity. I wasn't a criminal, I never had been and I'd never contemplated prison. Someone told me that a defeatist attitude in court will only lead to one place and I had to be aware of this at all times.

Then the jury came in and we were off. The CID geezer was called up, and he and the barrister reconstructed my arrest interview. The CID bloke played himself and the barrister played me as they read a transcript. It was a struggle to work out whether this was a courtroom or a fucking pantomime.

Here's my own reconstruction.

CID: *Tell us why you did it, Mr Turbo.*

TERRY: *Did what?*

CID: *Why you beat him senseless.*

TERRY: *He was already senseless.*

CID: *Are you saying you did do it?*

TERRY: *Course I didn't fucking do it. Iks is a fucking liar and a fucking cokehead con man. It could have been any one of a hundred people because no one likes him. The only reason he's saying it's me is because I kept phoning him up about it and called him on the day he got smashed up.*

Then Iks took the stand. He came across exactly how I'd described him, twitching like Bill Oddie in an aviary, scratching away and all jittery. I doubt anyone in the room didn't think he was a cokehead within seconds of seeing him. Hopefully, they'd start to believe my word because of my accurate description.

Best of all was when Jayne ambushed him over his call a few days before the trial, when he'd demanded ten grand not to turn up in court. He was stunned, frozen, not knowing how to react or what to say and the great thing was that he didn't have to say a thing because his expression said everything. He was caught out and was fucked.

When I was called up, I was in the dock for a full day. Now *that* was stressful. You cannot relax because you are being cross-examined, being scrutinised by the barristers and asked the same questions over and over to highlight any inconsistencies while the judge and the jury listen to everything you say and watch your body language. I was trying to convey that, although I was a little bit rough around the edges, I hadn't committed the offence I was accused of. If I showed any hint of a 'bad' side to my personality at any time, the jury would assume I was a bad person. The slightest mistake can cost you dearly. I was absolutely exhausted when I was finally allowed to step down. I'd done all I could to convince everyone in there of my innocence and there was absolutely no way of second-guessing how well I had performed. 'Performance' seems an odd way of terming it, but that's exactly how I see it. Being in court is like being on stage.

The CID guy was called in. He told the court that I hadn't phoned to put the record straight about the car and where I was, but had phoned to confess all.

Was he for real?

He was certainly trying to give that impression. Jayne pointed out that I was pleading 'not guilty' to all charges, and asked why I'd phone the CID to confess my guilt? More to the point . . . why would I do that when I knew all calls were either recorded or a precise record of them were kept?

Ah . . . that precise record. If you say something so incriminating in court, you need to back it up with evidence. Jayne asked for the recording of the conversation to be played or a detailed description of it to be circulated.

Silence.

Mr CID had really fucked up. He 'couldn't find his notes'. At all. Yes . . . unfortunately, even though he wrote it all down word for word, he must have put it somewhere so safe that not even he could locate the said document.

'That's very convenient,' said Jayne.

The CID geezer had nothing to say. There was nothing he *could* say.

When Stuart was called up to speak on my behalf, the issue of his convictions was always going to come up. He addressed the court, saying he had been wrongly convicted and had always stood by this claim. He said he was an innocent man, and so was I. It was great that he was still prepared to speak the truth even when he'd been warned not to – something he knows I appreciate a lot.

My star witness was Frances, who was there to knock down the bollocks about the car we'd all supposedly arrived in. She took no shit from anyone and had a fucking huge pair of balls for a woman. Fully in control, she said, 'I had the car that day. Here's the receipt from the garage, stating when mine was being serviced. Here's a list of people I met in those days I had the car, who will all tell you I was driving it.'

On the last day of the trial, both barristers summed up their cases for the jury. The prosecuting barrister went through a story that no one in their right mind would believe if they'd seen it at the cinema, let alone for real.

Jayne commented that it sounded like the plot to a Tarantino film gone wrong. There were no fingerprints or other forensic evidence to link me to the scene, because I hadn't been there. There were no independent witnesses, and my mobile phone signal wasn't pinging back from Oxford, for the same reason. There was no CCTV footage from any of the garages along the way, where I would have had to refuel, and there was no motorway footage showing my little old Toledo trundling up north. They didn't have any, because no such footage existed. Jayne asked the jury to think about it logically and sensibly, because there was a lot at stake here. She left them to answer this question: Would one man drive from Camberley to Plumstead, pick up three other men, drive to Oxford in broad daylight to beat up someone, while all wearing knuckle-dusters, because of a three hundred pound debt, and leave empty-handed?

If their answer was yes, I would get sent down for a five-stretch.

I looked every one of them in the eye as she asked the question.

It was almost too tempting to answer it for them and go off on one, telling them what a dishonest geezer Iks was.

The jury were ushered out to make their decision and returned a couple of hours later. The spokesman told the court that they'd been unable to reach a decision.

I wanted to shout, 'You're fucking joking!'

How could they not see the facts? If I had wanted him fucked-over, *I would NOT have done it myself.* How hard was that to grasp?

The judge told them to base their decision on the *evidence.* 'Look at what little proof there is to suggest that Mr Turbo is guilty. If you think there is enough evidence to place him at the scene of the crime, then fucking say so.'

Or words to that effect.

He said he'd accept a majority decision, and if that didn't come in he would go to a retrial, and sent them back out.

After an hour, they were back with a decision.

It was ten to two in favour of 'not guilty'.

I don't think I've been as happy – those five years may as well have been the death penalty and not guilty meant I was free of this nightmare that had lasted the best part of a year.

The puzzling part was how two of them actually thought I'd done it. But fuck them.

Jayne Terry stood up after the verdict to ask for my costs to be paid. The judge ruled that if I'd told the cops everything, and assisted properly in the arrest and interview, it wouldn't even have gone to trial so I could stick it up my arse. Fair enough.

The money was a side issue, anyway; this nightmare had come close to costing me everything so, in the scheme of things, a few grand was easy to live with. Don't get me wrong, five grand was five grand, but five years would have been a killer. I'd lost nine months of my life, and, temporarily, my sanity, but I was out of there.

It was alarming that some prick could make such a story up and so many people take it seriously enough to bring to court and waste a lot of time and money. They should have done *him*.

Once out of court, I took a deep breath and filled my lungs full of fresh air. I'd come to hate Oxford but it wasn't the surroundings I was bothered about, it was the fact that I was free. When your whole life has been jeopardised you learn to appreciate it more. I rounded up some of my closest friends to go on a massive bender. Hannah, my girlfriend at the time, stood by me through it all and was a tower of strength for me.

I'd seen off the tax and VAT people and now the police and the courts, and I'd been in the right, too.

I got on the phone and ordered a limousine stocked with champagne and we travelled in style for the whole weekend. going clubbing and celebrating my freedom.

Two and a half days later, the celebrating was out of my system. It was a huge comedown to assess what I'd been through. I couldn't sit around and dwell on what could have happened, though. Thinking about *what ifs* is counter productive; you need to learn from stuff that happens and move on. I'd certainly learnt from this one: If anything bad can happen, it may well do. And it will happen when you least expect it to. It was like karma – I'd done some things in the past that I'm not too proud of, and some things that no one will ever know about – and this was payback, a wake-up-call. If I'd gone to prison, it would have been my past catching up with me. This time I'd not been guilty, but in the past maybe I wasn't so innocent. Now the slate was clean and it was time to start again, only this time one mistake could be my last.

It was time to stop fucking around and realise that there was so much going on that I could easily mess up. To have the threat of losing everything like that really makes you look at how you live your life. I gave up every hedonistic trait as if I just put them in a bag and threw them out. No more alcohol, no more silliness and no more surrounding myself with the kinds of people who could potentially get me thrown into jail. I felt I'd been given a chance to put everything behind me, like it was all or nothing.

But fuck it. It was over, and I'd won. And, fuck me, what a relief.

HIGHS AND LOWS

I've had some fucking great nights through being a promoter.

I'm no Brad Pitt, but women flock to you. Some of them love the money they think you're making. I mean, look at all the women Mick Hucknall's shagged. Do you think it's because of his toned body and good looks? He's got curly ginger hair for fuck's sake – he gets laid all the time because he's rich and famous. Others like the red carpet treatment, like being walked in without paying, taken to the VIP area. Some get turned on by knocking around with a geezer who employs a pack of wild animals as his door team. Funny people, women. Some of them, anyway.

Obviously, it was great – good-looking girls falling over themselves to fuck you without so much as the hassle of a chat up line needed. Who wouldn't love that? I pulled some absolutely stunning birds but I never believed my own publicity. There were so many hangers-on, and rave groupies, and I loved having a Jack the Lad image, but I knew it was fuck all to do with me, really – if I'd kept going to the same old bars in Camberley like all my mates from the Old Dean, I'd have pulled the same clapped-out old boilers everyone else did.

It wasn't just me, obviously. DJs had birds all over the place. They'd shag anything. They didn't know when their career would be over, so they got it while they could. I remember one was shagging a 16-year-old and then used to fuck her mum when she came to pick her up. It was mental. This one DJ used to brag all the time about how many women he was doing up and down the country and then his missus turned up one night and he was like a different person. He didn't have time to warn anyone, so he was paranoid all night in case someone dropped him in the shit. I was just amazed that anyone would marry the fucker.

And don't think doormen weren't at it, either. Think about all the times you've been to a bar in your town and the doormen are surrounded by good-looking women – in a rave they were surrounded by them for 10 hours, and a lot of the birds were gagging for it. Ecstasy does that to them. I didn't mind who or what they were shagging, as long as it didn't affect their work. A doorman who was banging some slapper over the bins round the back of the club when a fight was kicking off inside was an unemployed doorman. It was that simple.

In my younger days, it was amazing because the scene really did have that hedonistic sex, drugs and rock'n'roll feel, with fighting as an extra bonus if you wanted it. Being at a rave definitely increased your chances because the women were so sexually expressive. You just had to look at their clothes to suss out what they'd be like in the sack, and they answer was usually as filthy as fuck. At raves, you could approach women without fear; women could flirt with you and not feel intimidated that you'd demand anything from them – that was the freedom of expression in there and there was never any pressure to go home with someone at the end of the night. There were groupies all the time and I could still be with them now if I wanted to be. But I was never really a complete dirty stop-out because, deep down, I was looking for the right bird to come along and I was never going to find her at one of my raves.

Most of my relationships used to last six months to a year tops.

I met Sarah – Jade's mum – at an event 1994. We went out together for around two years, on and off, and split up before Jade was born. We'd already realised we had nothing in common at all. She just wanted to go out and get off her head and I was working, business was good and getting better, and I couldn't just leave it all for the sake of going out.

Hannah was another raver – and she was raving mad, too. I mean, *proper* mad – she'd been in the loony bin before and didn't think it was worth telling me.

She was the one I was with during the court case – when she was like a rock for me – and I very nearly ended up buying a house with her. That was a lucky escape.

I had a mate and his bird living with me at the time. Whenever I came back from work, I'd find them all monged out in bed. My mate was into drugs, it was no secret, although I didn't know he was a serious fucking addict. I also didn't know he owed people money. One day I listened to my home phone answer machine and it was full of messages from some thug saying he wanted his money and was going to come round and cut him up if he didn't pay.

I got in touch with the bloke and sorted the money out, and told him to stop phoning up because it was my house. That night, I had a right go at my mate – a rave promoter cannot live in a house full of druggies. This bloke was supposed to be a fucking window cleaner – another one – so I told him to get his act together or sling his hook.

He didn't do either, and things went from bad to worse. Hannah phoned me on my way home one morning.

'I've had a fucking row with your mate,' she was screaming. 'I'm going to kill him.'

I was only half a mile away. 'Look,' I said, 'just calm down. I'll be there in a minute and we can sort everything out.'

When I got there I found she'd tried to smash my brief-case open because (jokingly, officers) I'd told her there was a gun in it. Well, I'd thought it would stop her snooping around. I never thought she'd try to get the (non-existent) fucker out to top my mate. I got between them and told him to pack up and fuck off. Then I tried to calm Hannah down. She'd completely flipped out, to the point where, hours later, I couldn't go to sleep. I thought in that frame of mind she'd attack me, imagining I was my junkie mate. Eventually, I coaxed her into taking the dog for a walk and as soon as she was gone I phoned her old man.

'Hannah's acting very strangely,' I said.

'Oh, no. Not again,' he said. That was when he told me about her stint in the nuthouse, and *that* was when I arranged for the locks to be changed.

My next girlfriend was a Page Three model who used to make a living as a Baby Spice tribute. It was great at first but she ended up more like Scary Spice and then the newest member, Pissed Spice. Wilf Pine told me this once. 'When you realise that all women are mad, you'll be fine.' I was beginning to think he had a point. I reckon I had some sort of nutty bird attraction device in my head. And they were usually deranged psychopaths or druggies, or both. I don't mean they were crack-heads or shooting up heroin, I mean all they wanted to do was go out Thursday, Friday, Saturday and Sunday and get E-d up.

I can't say it was unpredictable. I suppose it was like hitting on a bird in an AA meeting – you pretty much know what to expect if you suggest a few vodkas.

If I'd been a pill-head, that kind of relationship would have suited me down to the ground. But I'd moved on from that shit a long time ago. All I wanted to do when I got home at around eight in the morning was sleep. Call me old fashioned if you like, but sitting up for a few more hours smoking puff and talking bollocks had no appeal. That's where a lot of my arguments with women started.

Me: 'Why can't you just go to bed like any other normal person?'

Her: 'I am a normal person. I just want to smoke this spliff, have another couple of beers and chill out.'

Me: 'But it's 10am and you've been up for 48 hours straight. That is not normal.'

Her: 'Oh, fuck off!'

Louise was different to the others. On the surface. We were together for around three years and I met her at… well, where the fuck do you think I met her? A modelling agency phoned me one day to say these birds were coming to the rave that night, and could we put them on our models' guest list.

'The what?'

'The models' guest list,' she repeated.

'Er . . . right,' I said. 'Who are they?'

She rattled off a couple of names and said they were in a current issue of Loaded or something.

We created a models' guest list – all of two names on it – and I nipped out for a copy of the mag. Fuck me, they were fit. I was looking forward to greeting and chaperoning these young ladies personally. Nice one – gorgeous models in my club, what more could I ask for? Drunk ones, Terry? Good point, let's get a few bottles of shampoo in.

I slipped by the models' VIP area that night to introduce myself.

It was the usual tale of model meets Terry, model falls in love with Terry. She did more than that, she fucking moved in, and it all went wrong from there.

She was a working woman, and she wanted to do things, have her own place, be independent, go travelling. I think she maybe felt overshadowed by me being Mr Music Promoter. She certainly felt she had to pay her own way. We'd go out to dinner and she was used to being the breadwinner and in control, going halfers or trying to pay, which I wouldn't allow. (Mind you, all this 'paying my own way' shit went by the by when we took a flight on Concorde to New York and back to Paris. If you're wondering whether we joined the mile high club – we didn't. It was on my priority list, though.) She couldn't come to terms with being in a relationship with another strong character. After around nine months, she gave up modelling because there were certain things she didn't want to do. I know what you're thinking – she wasn't that kind of model. Honest. It was clean – very clean, in fact, it was a soap ad that she refused to do. Fair enough, models can pick and choose... but this job was worth £35,000.

She got very jealous, too. She'd phone me at work and demand to know the names of all the women that she could hear in the background. Eh? All two thousand of them, love? She had bigger issues than a homeless magazine seller, this one.

Don't get me wrong – she had her good points. Apart from the two on her chest, she was good with ideas. It was Louise who suggested trying out some different events. She was well into her music and had her own decks, and she came up with Rave Nation and R'n'B Nation. They never went as big as One Nation or Garage Nation, but they were reasonably successful – new ideas like that needed to be explored and never written off until they turned to shit. But the way, after we set these up, I had a run-in with the Ministry of Sound because they put out an album called Rave Nation. I phoned them up to have a go and got passed around every department. I sent them a legal letter in the end – they knew I meant business and settled up by paying my legal fees and a few thousand on top as compensation.

I knew Louise had to go when she started smashing up a brand new fitted wardrobe which cost me a lot of money. I got home to find her crying on the floor surrounded by bits of wood. When I went to comfort her, she tried to stab me with a screwdriver. I nearly shit a brick – it was the last thing I was expecting. Because it was such a surprise, my immediate reaction was I slapped her. Quite hard. In fact, I unintentionally sparked her out and then panicked even more because she'd turned me, albeit accidentally, into a wife-beater. She woke up and tried to do it again. It was like the final scene in *Fatal Attraction* – a film which gave us the term 'bunny boiler.'

After calming her down it was definitely time to give her the P45 before something serious happened to me or her.

I seemed to spend half my life watching my back in case my latest girlfriend had a carving knife in her hand, or apologising to people for something she'd done or said, or waiting for her to come down from whatever cocktail of evil narcotics she'd snorted or swallowed. But like all men, I was slow to learn.

Every time I met someone, I'd say to my mum, 'This is the one. She's great. She's just what I'm looking for.'

And she never was. I went out with actresses, models, ravers, secretaries, women who had their own companies, women with multiple personalities, every one of them nutty . . . and each time something would go wrong, usually something associated with mood swings, temper tantrums or attempted murder.

I remember sitting round my mum's house and saying, 'Mum, why the fuck can't I find a nice normal girl who wants to settle down and live a normal life? *Are* there any normal birds in the world?'

She looked at me. 'Terry,' she said, 'You're going to raves to meet girls . . . what do you expect? They're rave sluts. They want to get off their heads, go clubbing, sleep around. Going for dinner doesn't bother them. If they're hungry they'll eat something but it could be a McDonalds, it doesn't have to be dinner in a Michelin star restaurant.'

As usual, she was annoyingly right.

I hadn't found the right bird because I was looking in the wrong place.

Finally, I found her. Her name was Maxine, and, funnily enough, I wouldn't have met her if it wasn't for the rave scene.

Within minutes of meeting her, I knew she was the one for me. Sometimes you just do. The mistake I'd made in the past was that I *wanted* every girl to be the one – like I was searching for someone that didn't exist. I was blinkered. She didn't exist because I hadn't met her until I met Max. After that, everything was right... everything was different.

We met in July 2001, in a Sharon and Tracey nightclub. She was with her best mate, Russ Abbot's daughter, Erica. By coincidence, or fate, I was there with a mate who knew Erika. As they were talking, I asked if they want a drink. Erika wanted champagne and Max said, 'He's a doorman, he can't afford that.'

She was uncomfortable about me paying because she assumed I was a bouncer like my mate – from her reaction, I knew she was considerate and caring. We got talking . . . it turned out that she worked in property and I mentioned I owned a bit here and there, we got on well and exchanged cards. A week later I was passing the club again and decided to go in on the off-chance, wondering if she was there. And she was. She'd already said to her friends, 'Wouldn't it be funny if that mad skinhead guy is here?'

We got talking again and I said I'd phone her the next day. She was a bit apprehensive, so I told her to come round to my place where it would be more relaxed and we could just chill out. She was driving round for ages thinking she'd got the address wrong, because it was full of smart houses that a 'doorman' wouldn't live in. She phoned me, which was good: just the fact that she had her own car and could operate a mobile phone reassured me she wasn't just another nutty bird and that, if I played my cards right, she might not stab me. I directed her to 'a big white house with brand new CL500 with German number plates in the drive – you can't miss it.' The CL had just come out and as you couldn't get them over here, I'd had it imported. Of course, Max thought I must be looking after the house for someone. That was always a plus-point. I had all these pictures around the place – various Kray funerals and other gangster stuff – plus bullet proof vests lying around, holdalls . . . it couldn't have looked any dodgier if I'd staged the whole thing. We spent ages just chatting, and I realised I was falling for her, big-time. She was very normal, she came from a nice family – her mum and dad have been married for 30 years, and were sensible, self-made people, with great stability – and she wasn't into that clubby drug shit. Amazingly, she said she wanted to get married, have kids and live a normal existence. *Where've you been all my life?*, I thought.

Don't get me wrong, there were people a lot worse off than me, but if you come from a broken home, and your mum has to work, and there's no money, and your old man knocks you about when you're young and then leaves, and then your mum's boyfriends come home pissed and they do it to you, too, and you get bullied at school . . . somewhere, subconsciously, you crave normality, the family thing you never had. You want to be a proper father, part of a proper unit.

We started dating, and people were amazed, because of my gangster reputation and also because we appeared to be as different as chalk and cheese. The thing was, the Terry Turbo Maxine met was the real one – not the geezer in a rave punching the fuck out of some mugger's face.

It was a bit of a whirlwind romance – in no time at all, I was introduced to her parents. When I met them, I thought her dad was just like me – down to earth and a decent geezer. Her mum was posh – when she first heard about me, she said to Max, 'I didn't pay to send you to the best school in the country so you could go out with a skinhead doorman' – but what did I expect? I knew she'd warm to me and she did. Weirdly, they lived in a house I'd admired for years. It was unbelievable. Years before, I used to walk down this millionaire's road and pass the place each time, wondering who lived there. The perimeter wall was about a mile long and the owners were all I'd ever thought about on that walk. It was too bizarre to be sat there in the place and going out with the girl who lived there.

After a month, we got engaged and moved in together. It sounds like we rushed in maybe, but we both knew it was the right thing to do. We're happy, there's no madness and we do everything a normal couple should. Neither of us ever used to go to the club we met at – it just happened that Max was there those two times . . . I reckon it was fate and I'm glad I acted on my impulses.

There are so many things about Max that attracted me to her. Being such a positive influence on me, she taught me how to look at things differently and it's something I'm grateful for. In my rave days, I was arrogant and single-minded – she brought me out of that mindset. I still have my opinion and will argue with anyone if I know I'm right, but now I can take things on board now and listen to a balanced argument without losing my rag.

Max is different to all of the other girls I've known. She's got class, morals, principles, everything. I could be relaxed going out with her in company because I knew she wouldn't show me up by being off her head. That's where her good upbringing set her apart from the others – she can get on with anyone and introduced me to some very influential business-people. These are not influential in the *I was a gangster* sense, I mean people with real power who live in £20 million houses and were never likely to do their networking at an unlicensed boxing event. These kind of people know someone like Max wouldn't be with me if I was a cock. She's my soul mate, my best mate and the woman I'll spend the rest of my life with. Max kept me on the straight and narrow and has always been my sounding board for everything I do.

Back at work, things were going brilliantly, and we began to win awards.

The best thing you can ever be given for your work is an award. Alright, that's bollocks. The best thing you can be given is a £100,000 pay rise, a new company Merc and the best-looking secretary in the firm on her knees in front of you in the boss's office. But if that's not available, an award comes close. I bet even the kids in McDonald's who get named Floormopper of the Week™ feel proud of themselves for being noticed. When we started getting recognition from the industry, it felt awesome. I'd proved a few people wrong – like the guys behind The Flying Squad, who'd said I wouldn't last 10 minutes – and shown a few others they'd been wrong to fuck me around. If you see Phil and Mick from Tottenham, or Car-Ringer Mark and Andy, or Murray fucking Taylor, do give them my best. And ask them how many awards they've got on their mantelpieces.

Our events were good, too. Fuck that, they were great. Our promotional material was always top notch, we spent far more than we had to on lights and lasers and sound, we booked the best DJs around and my Team always, always, always did whatever it took to keep our punters as safe as possible. What swung it for us, though, was the club tours. I'm sure that was largely why we won the awards. We were running One Nation events all around the country – as many as 20 a month. If you add in the bigger events we ran ourselves, and the seasons in Ibiza and Ayia Napa, we were giving a million clubbers a year a good time, every time. And people have to fucking sit up and take notice of that.

Kiss FM held the Hardcore Dance Awards at the Camden Palace in 1998 and we got the award for Best Club Promoter: One Nation was everywhere, and there was no real choice. This geezer called Um Foo Foo (don't ask) was heart heart-broken when he had to give me the award because he wanted it. He was gutted. He used to do the Kiss FM in Ibiza thing and Kiss FM always won their own awards. (Ha, ha . . . only kidding!)

Best fucking Promoter! Not just a half-decent promoter, a good one or even the second best in the whole country – I was crowned *the* best. In all the land. Let me tell you, it felt pretty fucking good.

Me and Um Foo Foo had a bit of a history. I used to wind him up all the time and he didn't like it at all. He phoned me up before the event and said, 'You've won, you cunt.'

His real name – well, it wasn't his real name, I'm sure, but you know what I mean – was Funky. He ran Elevation and I had a few run-ins with him. We never had a fight or anything, it was just one of those personality clash things – I had one and he didn't. One time he'd accused me of not handing out his flyers properly, and it had all spiralled from there. We Christened him Um Foo Foo after one of the Eddie Murphy stand up shows from the '80s, where Eddie does a sketch about marrying 'some dumb black bitch on a zebra, called Um Foo Foo'. Because Funky was a huge black geezer and a bit wet behind the ears, the name stuck to him. There was no serious malice intended but people saw how much it wound him up, so they'd all join in. He didn't know why he was called it and probably doesn't know to this day, which is what made it all the more fun. Out in Ibiza, I primed everyone to go to his events and ask him, 'Are you Um Foo Foo?'

Next day, he'd phone me up in a rage. 'You fucking cunt!' he'd shout. 'Stop telling people to call me silly names!'

'What do you mean, calling you silly names? What are they calling you?' would be my innocent reply.

There would be a pause. 'They're calling me Um Foo fucking Foo.'

I'd have to hang up, pissing my pants, knowing that I'd made him say the name.

He went to a World Dance rave and there were about 70 people outside flying, absolutely loads of promoters. Someone started whispering, 'Um Foo Foo,' and then someone else did, and it carried on from there, like a low murmur. Um Funky Foo Foo heard it and turned to see who it was, but he was surrounded by everyone and nobody was giving themselves away . . . 'Um Foo Foo, Um Foo Foo,' it was fucking priceless.

'Stop calling me Um Foo fucking Foo you cunts!'

Anyway, fuck him.

The next award was *The Knowledge* Drum'n'Bass Awards which were held at Hammersmith Palais the following year. I got Best Large Venue Promoter award for One Nation.

OK, so two consecutive years suggests it wasn't a fluke the first time. I was like James Cameron when he won his Oscar for Titanic, bursting to shout, 'I'm king of the worrrrld!' But I would have looked up my own arse as much as he did.

In 2000, *The Knowledge* Awards were sponsored by Red Stripe, so with some genius wordplay, they became *The Knowledge*-and-Red Stripe Awards. One Nation was Best Venue Promoter. Too fucking right we were!

Hammersmith Apollo played host to the UK Garage Awards in 2000 and Garage Nation was nominated for Best Promoter, but a company called Exposure won it. What a load of old bollocks that was. I was angry at the time: we were top dogs in Ibiza by now, we were doing Ayia Napa, over 20 clubs up and down the country every month, big events and all the tape packs. We had the highest profile in the country and Exposure, who did a wanky little club night at The Coliseum once a month on a Saturday night and never set up shop anywhere outside

London, walked off with Best Promoter? It was a fucking farce, and that's not sour grapes. If I thought they deserved it, I'd say so.

In 2001, Brixton Academy hosted a big ceremony for the UK Garage Awards with loads of celebs and music people and TV cameras. We won Best Garage Promoter with Garage Nation and it proved our point from last year's joke. I went there with Max and we had an amazing time. She parked her Mercedes SLK out the front of the venue and we got out – her in a fur coat, me in a gold Versace suit, like something out of a Snoop video. I got absolutely slaughtered on Morgan's Spice rum and we left in the early hours, me clutching my award and Max keeping me steady. As we left, a load of scumbags tried to rush the doors, with loads of other hoodies on BMXs hanging around waiting to join in. Someone had been carjacked, there was a lot of shouting and yelling and Max was frightened. I said, 'Fuck it . . . if they want to have a go I'll smash them with this.' The award had lots of sharp edges and was going to be my weapon of choice. But no-one touched us. They must have thought they were being set up with some sort of police sting operation . . . Max in her fur coat and diamonds, me in a gold suit walking around in Brixton at 3am. It was a bit weird.

Winning awards for my events was the crowning glory.

One Nation touched a lot of people – we were the best and won awards for being the best. Getting that kind of recognition made it all worthwhile.

As well as all the ups, though, there were plenty of downs along the way.

Ironically, the biggest disaster happened the year we got Best Venue Promoter – the year 2000, Millennium Night.

There'd been masses of hype and hysteria about the Millennium. I read about it all; it was a once-in-a-lifetime thing and surely we ought to be in there, doing something big? The only thing was, I'd done a couple of New Year dos before and they never were really all that big for us. We made a bit here, lost a bit there, generally broke even. The problem was, the superclub nights – like Ministry's rave for 20,000 people and stuff – would be on and, once a year, people wanted to go out to something really big, not the usual 2,000 or 3,000-strong parties. It's human nature: if you've been to One Nation or Garage Nation at The Rex, or Brixton Academy, or Roller Express, six times already that year, you're going to want to go somewhere unusual for the biggest night of the century: you want to be somewhere the size of a small town.

The other problem with New Year's Eves, generally, was, everyone else was on double bubble – the DJs wanted double, the venues wanted double, the security, the lighting and sound . . . everyone except you, because you just couldn't charge enough to make double for you, too. The situation was even worse for the Millennium: the talk was of doormen on a grand a night, for fuck's sake.

Even worse, there was the so-called Millennium Bug knocking around. This was a big media scare: the internal clocks in many computers were going to go haywire at midnight, apparently, and the chances were that everything with a chip in it was going to go down. The power supply was quite likely to be among them, supposedly, and you can't have a party without electricity. So we'd need big generators outside on standby in case.

We needed to be charging £100 a ticket to cover costs and make decent money ourselves, and I thought that was going to be a lot to ask.

In fact, the more I thought about it, the more reasons there were to avoid Millennium Night like the plague.

I said to Jason, 'Look, I'm worried. I'm not convinced. Why don't we forget it and do New Year's Day instead? We could call it 'Payback' and charge 12 or 15 quid?'

'Yeah,' says Jase. 'Good idea, sorted.'

So I booked three clubs for New Years Day.

We'd had a fantastic year in '99, made some serious money.

Everything was looking really sweet. Then some club owner rung me up. 'Tel,' he said. 'What you doing for New Year's Eve? Only, no-one's booked us . . . so why don't you?'

I said I'd think about it and I started mulling it over. It had been on the news that Blair was relaxing the licensing laws. I was thinking about a hook, and one came to me: how about doing England's first 24-hour rave? Which sounds great. If you're a loony.

I said to Jase, 'Look, we'll do the Jan 1 things but we'll just do a 24-hour One Nation as well . . . we'll start on New Year's Eve.'

I started doing some figures, trying to work out the minimum we could charge. It came out at 80 quid a ticket, which was sharp intake of breath time. I needed to have a think.

A week later, someone else came up to me and said, 'What you doing with Dreamscape on New Year's Eve?' This was Murray Beetson's old thing.

Then another geezer comes up to me and says, 'Tel, I've got Streatham Ice Rink for Millennium Night... it's gonna be huge, you gotta do it.'

We sat round a table and thought about it. Dreamscape at the Pleasure Rooms we could do cheap, at 50 quid, the One Nation at Club UN in Tottenham would take care of itself and the Garage Nation do would be great . . . that crowd were always loaded, drinking bottles of Cristal and Hennessy and all that bollocks. I worked out that if we filled them all up we'd make fucking fortunes. I'd take home the best part of a quarter of a million and Jase would have taken a hundred grand. I looked at him. 'You know what,' I said. 'We've gotta do it. There's only one Millennium and if we don't, someone else will and we'll spend all next year wondering why we bottled it.'

He's like, 'Yeah, fuck it. We're in.'

I ordered the flyers and started planning.

So now we've gone from having three dos on New Year's Day to three on New Year's Eve, having forgotten all the fucking reasons not to touch it with a bargepole. Somehow, all the logical, sensible thinking about what to do and what not to do had gone out of the window.

We got some great flyers sorted, arranged the generators, got great line-ups booked, drafted in extra security and did all the other million and one behind the scenes jobs that were needed to get everything on the road. Then we sat back, and waited for the tickets to start selling.

And we fucking waited.

Three days before the night, we did a ring round of the shops. We'd sold 100 tickets for One Nation, 60 for Garage Nation and Dreamscape was about half done.

'Jay,' I said. 'We've fucked up.'

He looked pretty fucking glum.

To make matters worse, loads of other people had now decided to do New Year's Day parties, and they were all sold out.

'If anything ever looks that good on paper again, it ain't,' I said.

Right. Mourning over. Next question: how the fuck are we going to come out of this alive?

First, we still record all the nights and sell tape packs, really flog them to death. After all, it's still a Millennium Night party, people are going to want a record of that to listen to years later.

Second, everyone's getting chopped: the DJs, the doormen, the venues . . . everyone.

I rang all the venue owners up. 'Listen,' I said. We've sold no tickets. You wanted 50k for your venue . . . you're getting 10k.'

Next I rang the doormen. I had more sympathy here – these were my mates. But I'd been good to them over the years. If they ever needed favours doing, cash loans, whatever, I'd been there for them. Now I needed them. I knew they'd come through and they did. They were all on the usual £100.

I didn't call the DJs. They'd been expecting 2k an hour. They were coming down to £200. They'd find that out when they arrived, or else they'd never turn up.

Fuck me, it was bad.

My then bird Louise was running Dreamscape, I was running One Nation, I had another guy in charge of Garage Nation and Jase was flying around DJing.

Dreamscape, we had 800 people in, in a venue for 1,000. So that wasn't too bad.

Garage Nation, we had 400 people in a 3,000 venue. Shit.

One Nation, we had 300 in a 3,000 venue. Total shit.

They both looked terrible. The atmosphere was from awful to non-existent.

We closed Garage Nation down and told everyone to get over to One Nation, which made a bit of a difference, a few more bodies in. But no-one had a great night. And if you were there . . . sorry. We overreached ourselves, got too ambitious, too greedy. Feet back on the earth time.

The only good thing you could say is that *everyone* was quiet, so it wasn't a total slap in the face for us, our brands and our promotional expertise. People had stayed in or gone down the pub, basically.

True to form, every single fucking DJ who came in the club, their first question was, Where's my money?

I said, 'You're not getting your fucking money.'

Cue the moaning.

I said, 'Come here . . . look at that.' I showed them a few kids mooching about on an empty dancefloor. 'How the fuck can I give you your money? If you don't like it, fuck off and you'll never play for me again.'

They still moaned like cunts, though most accepted it with bad grace. One or two gave it the really big one and I never used them again.

Actually, while I'm on the fucking subject: DJs.

A lot of them got wanky once they got halfway famous. Not all of them – take Jay Kaye or Slipmatt for example; they're both brilliant geezers and very popular DJs. Neither of them turned into J-Lo as soon as they got fans. I could say the same about 10 or 20 other DJs and MCs. All the other fuckers were just cunts, and if you think about how many were in circulation, that's a lot of cunts. In the early days, they'd got something like £50 an hour, which isn't bad when you consider that a teacher's average hourly rate 10 years on is about a third of that. Now – talk about fucking inflation – tell me if this isn't fucking ridiculous? After a few years, some of these boys were asking for more like £1,000 to £1,500 an hour. How does that work? It was all just made up as they went along. Once they started demanding more money, you had to pay. They could hold you to ransom and they knew it. Instead of 20 bookings a week they would do five and put their price up. When they realised people would still pay, the DJs thought, *Fuck it. I'll still do 20 at the same extortionate rate.* And it got worse. After they put all their prices up, they wanted money for the tapes we sold as well. We were doing them a favour by selling the tapes in the first place because it was a promotional tool for all concerned, as we always had an advert for our next event on the back. They were also a good safety net, as I've said: if we didn't have a good night and maybe lost five grand or so, the tapes would make that money back and allow us to carry on. There were a few, like Goldie and Adam F, who got really arsey about being recorded. For fuck's sake, they were paid two grand and a grand, respectively: for that kid of dough, I'll fucking run a tape, thanks – especially while you're standing there drinking my champagne all night. I told them that if it was a problem, fuck off and don't come back. Goldie was alright about it in the end, but this Adam F geezer took it too far. He actually phoned my mum and had a go at her. I knew right away who it was on the line, and when I heard mum say, 'Don't talk to me like that,' I grabbed the receiver off her.

'I will smash your fucking face in for that, you little prick,' I said. 'This is how it is. I taped you. It happens to everyone. If you don't like it, fuck you. I won't book you again.'

He said fine, I said fine and I put his name on the flyer regardless, just to piss him off.

Another one was Mickey Finn – the only DJ I ever came to

blows with. This idiot didn't want to be recorded unless there was more money upfront. Out of all the difficult ones I remember, he was top of the list and fell out with half the promoters he worked for at one time or another. There were so many other DJs bigger than him, and he was acting like he was a superstar. It started getting childish and a scrap was inevitable.

It was all petty attitudes and childish sulking with *I won't play for you anymore* if you ever questioned them. A few of them tried that approach so I told them to fuck off. Like with Adam F, I'd always put their name on the flyer, just to rattle their cage and wait for them to say something, so I could show them what a bad attitude really sounded like. It never happened. They'd always come running back.

Apart from most of them being part-geek, part-weasel, they had other problems. As the gangs and muggers began to cotton on a bit, they realised that DJs got paid in cash for their work. That meant that some of them got spun on their way home and even had their houses turned over. If they finished work at whatever o'clock, it's not like they're going to be able to go to the bank to make a deposit, so they have cash on them if you feel the urge to rob them. I know a few who were stopped in their car and more than a few who were robbed at home. They started buying metal cages to fix to their front door at home for protection. What sort of a way is that to live your life?

One night, a One Nation do at Brixton Academy, I had this geezer called MC Navigator who wanted to argue over money he was owed. Naturally, he had two others with him. I really couldn't be fucking bothered: he was getting fuck all out of me, but I didn't want anything to spoil my night – certainly not a prick like him.

The trouble had started after he double-booked himself with us and someone else. We'd booked him way ahead, flyers had been printed and distributed and his name was on them. Then he phoned to say he wouldn't be doing our show because he'd got a better offer for more money. I told him I'd get someone else to fill his slot. It was no big deal to me – this sort of shit was happening more often than not, so I was used to having to replace all these whingey little toss pots at the drop of a hat. I'm sure he was expecting me to beg him to do the gig and offer him more money. *Oh please, oh pleeeease MC Navigator. The event is ruined if you let us all down!* Yeah, right. Bye, bye.

On the night, his other booking got cancelled and he just turned up to do his set for us like it was the most normal thing in the world. I let him do it and afterwards he demanded twice the agreed fee. Well, you can guess where this is going. I told him to piss off, his mates started crowding in and it developed into a stand-off, with me, Felix and Jez Bailey staring the cunts down. Their bottle went. I turned to walk away and one of them, some twat calling himself Daddy Freddy, called after me. 'You lucky I don't have to make a call, man.'

Not very subtly, he was hinting they could have me whacked.

I turned round. 'Make whatever fucking calls you want, you cunt, but the best call you can make will be to the fucking hospital,' I said. 'Don't tell me how fucking lucky I am. If you want to call it on, then fucking call it on.'

The Kingpin collapsed like a burst balloon and the three of them navigated a sharp exit.

I was surprised I hadn't chinned him. Maybe I was growing up. Max was on the scene now: her influence was improving me.

Anyway, that's enough cunty DJ and MC stories.

Where was I? Millennium Night.

Worst night of my promoting life by a long way.

In the morning, me and Jase hugged each other and I went off in my car. I got a call that afternoon. He was still outside the venue. His car had broken down and he'd had to wait eight hours for the AA. Talk about a nightmare.

No-one earned any money. Even by chopping people, me and Jase lost about 100 grand between us. We made a bit back on the tape packs and we had a good Valentine's, but it took us a good six months to get back on track.

I was really gutted, sick as a pig. I couldn't believe I'd been that fucking stupid.

The New Year's Day parties that everyone else ran went down massive. If I'd have stuck with my original gut feeling, I'd have had 100k more in the bank, not less. So it was a 200k mistake, actually.

With the scene being so fickle, that night could easily have finished us. Punters might not have bothered coming back. Because we lived from one event to the other, each one had to make money to fund the next one and so on.

The thing I got from that night was finding out who my true friends were. Those people know who they are. They were prepared to go home empty-handed and had left their families behind to stand by me. When you're in the shit like that, your friends will be with you and with you forever.

One who wasn't going to be with me forever was Louise.

January 4, I'm moping around the house feeling like shit. She suddenly says, 'I wanna go shopping in the sales.'

I said, 'You what? Are you fucking stupid? What the fuck makes you think I wanna go and spend money after this? Are you fucking insane?'

That was the end of that relationship. I realised this bird had no fucking sense of reality. all she wanted to do was go out and get off her head and fuck around and spend money.

A few days later, we had the crying, the bitch and the wardrobe, and that was that.

A DECADE OF DANCE

We pulled it back after the Millennium fuck up and carried on going from strength to strength, but my mind was starting to wander into other areas. I'd been working in the industry for around 10 years now and other horizons were opening up.

I'd read a newspaper article back in 1999 about a psychic called Anne Walker who was very well known and highly regarded.

Our first meeting was after that Millennium fiasco. I was at a bit of a crossroads – I didn't know at the time if I could overcome this one. You know when you question everything you are doing? I was wondering whether it was worth carrying on in the rave scene and was looking for some answers as to where my future lay, and in what direction my life was headed. I wanted guidance. Spiritual matters had always fascinated me and I turned to Anne. It would be the first of many visits. I see her around once a year and have become good friends with her. It was Anne Walker (check out her books, *The Messenger and The Messiah* is unbelievable) who told me a book would be written about me. Mental, eh?

She was precise with everything she ever said to me. It was amazing. Over that time, I've been on spirituality courses and always look to Anne for reassurances that things I'm doing are the right ones for me and my family. She told me to listen to my heart and go with my gut instinct. If I felt I was being pulled one way – go with it, because it is probably the right way. It is no coincidence that you decide to become a singer or an actor or take a complete change of direction, it is because you are on a journey and that is a step along the way. It's destiny, and the key to accepting your destiny is having faith in yourself. This is why I went straight in to putting events on for three thousand people instead of three hundred. I've always aimed high and have never been prepared to settle for second best.

Then I did a past life regression with a lady called Vicky Yorke. This is going to sound nutty, I know – all I can say is, it's the truth. She took me under, and I found myself in America, around the time of the Great Depression. I was part of a Mafia family, and she took me through various stages of my life. I was married to a woman who was spookily like Max, who tried to get me out of my life of crime. She ended up being murdered and I retaliated by having her killers executed. I veered from giggling to crying to being so fucking angry I thought I was going to get up and kick the shit out of Vicky. Unable to talk properly and clenching my fists and teeth with rage, it was as real as any emotion I'd ever felt.

Yes, I know it sounds mad and I sure as hell don't know how to explain it. If it hadn't happened to me I'd be laughing, too. It was the most surreal experience ever. And it left me mentally drained and wiping away tears when she brought me out.

Since then, Vicky has put me under a few times. In one of these sessions, I was able – somehow – to ask God a question. I asked whether I'd been right to have my 'wife's' killers shot dead. The answer was, No, because it hadn't brought her back. Vicky asked how I felt about my 'wife'. I told her I'd always loved her and when she was killed it felt like my heart had been ripped out. That was a *real* emotion. I could feel my love for her and the sense of loss, and I have no way of explaining it.

At the end of the night, she had a full deck of 52 spiritual cards with random messages on, placed them face down on the table and asked me to pick the one that I felt most drawn to and look at it. Each of them carried a message – the one I picked up said *I love you now and I will love you forever and although you may not see me I am always with you.* It made my spine tingle because it was like my 'wife' was communicating to me, telling me everything was alright. I could hardly get the words out because I was so overwhelmed. I nearly broke down in tears. It was that emotional.

In black and white, I know this all sounds barmy, or completely made up. But I've been hypnotised in the past and when that happened I knew exactly what was going on. Past-life regression was different, because everything was unknown. I had the sessions recorded, so I know it happened; I can hear the anger and the despair at what was going on, my voice changing as I became 'younger'.

All I can say is, have a go at it yourself and then see.

From there, I developed an interest in reincarnation. Don't get me wrong, you won't see me in the West End dressed in peach-coloured robes singing Hare Krishna songs but I do feel we keep coming back to live on earth until we grow enough to go on to the next place, wherever the fuck that is.

I'd never been a church goer, but this new-found spiritual side started to affect me. That and the guns.

I had a do on at the Ministry of Sound one Christmas night in 2002, which got me thinking. We were on the door stopping all these geezers coming in with automatics, and they were saying, 'No way man ... we need our machines – there's other gangs inside wit' deirs.'

On Christmas-fucking-Day? Whatever happened to peace and good will? It was ridiculous.

This was the point where I started wanting out.

There was still the day to day shit to deal with, of course. We were owed a lot of money for tapes and tickets by a group of record shops owned by this big-time producer. He thought no one would fuck around with him and the unpaid invoices started mounting up.

I phoned them up and they said something along the lines of, 'Relax, you'll get paid.'

Unconvinced, I made a few enquiries and heard that they were all about to go under, so I called back. They said my invoices were being processed and it was obvious they were bullshitting me. Soon after my call, the shops started closing down. The ones in London went first because most of the people they owed were from there and they were less likely to chase him up north. Unless they were called Terry fucking Turbo. We took two cars up to Manchester and when the shopkeeper saw eight scary bastards walk in, he grabbed the phone.

'Unless you are ordering pizza, put the fucking phone down,' I said. (I was starving after the drive.) 'You took a liberty with me and now I'm going to take what you owe me. If you call the police, you'll get hurt.'

We cleaned the shop out – turntables, speakers, tape packs, records, t-shirts, records, the money out the till and there was barely room for us to fit back in the cars. I was driving with a Technics deck on my knee and we were laughing along, re-enacting the *Bohemian Rhapsody* scene from *Wayne's World* with me pretending to scratch along and remix it.

Everything was above board. I left a receipt with a list of everything we took which appeared to come to the six grand they owed me. All the gear was sold on and turned into cash and then a few days later, the guy himself phoned me. He said I had taken a liberty walking off with his gear because he was going to pay me.

'Let me stop you there, you lying little shit,' I said. '*You* are a cunt. You think you can fuck around with people because you've got money . . . well you can't. No one robs me.'

He started with *You don't know who I am and you don't know who I know*, and I could hardly hear him for yawning. He half-knew some gangsters, it turned out, and his plan was to go to them and tell them what I'd done.

'You tell them how much you tried to rob from me and then what I did to get it back. Then you can see if they want to get involved,' I said. I knew for a fact that no one would back him up. I never heard a dickie bird.

We'd started doing a lot of gigs at Brixton Academy. Brixton is scary enough through the daytime – gloomy and intimidating *and* you are smack-bang in the middle of all the scummy no-go areas, with other cess pits like Streatham and the Elephant and Castle just down the road. The venue backs on to the most horrible council estate imaginable – a rabbit warren of nastiness filled with druggies and criminals. We had to generalise and assume that anyone from there was potentially one of the cunts who was mugging my punters or selling drugs. I'm from a council estate myself, and I've always hated being labelled – but it was because I knew what went on that I could label them. Everyone from the council estate knew when One Nation had an event on, knew a load of kids from outside the area and not streetwise to Brixton would be coming, and would have money in their pockets – it was a one-night-opportunity to smash and grab into the early hours. Four and a half thousand kids with anything up to a hundred quid each and wearing designer gear always brought the muggers out. And believe me, that's exactly what happened. It was open season.

These were the kids we were protecting. They'd travel from all over to get to our events, the least we could do was offer them a safe night out. A lot of these punters were from nice areas and had good backgrounds. They'd never had to fight a gang in front of their own girlfriend, been robbed, mugged, had a knife held to their throat. From the tube stations to the venues, anything could happen. Muggers would surround them as soon as they got off the trains or wait in the shadows until the kids thought they were safe.

It was a constant battle, though not as bad as at some other places, funnily enough.

The main worry was these wannabes bringing in guns. It's no secret it's Yardie territory, gang warfare central, and we always felt like there was this threat looming over us: kind of, *we could smash them, we could bash them, but we'd have to answer to the guns of Brixton.* The place had a bad reputation and still has. If there's a gang from Brixton, people brick it

– just like they do with guys from places like Moss Side in Manchester.

The Academy is a big venue and despite the best efforts of the house security, there was no way anyone could keep all the guns out, so I had to assume everyone was carrying; I couldn't let my guard down. It was a constant headache: it seemed everyone other than my firm was working against me. At the Academy, we'd have fencing up and guard dogs on patrol because there were so many doorways round the back and so many places for people to hide. There had to be a constant presence in case anyone was watching, ready to rush the doors when we were outnumbered. This was the one venue that would always insist on their own people in the cash box. I made sure that my mum was in there with them, even though her contact with money and tickets was limited. At least she was there making sure everything was working as it should be. She had a suspicious mind.

I was always wary when leaving any venue in case I got jumped by a gang. There was a lot of money being taken each night – anywhere up to £40,000 in cash. To cut down the risk, I used to pay everyone with this money – the venue got weighed in with notes, the door team did, the DJs, the sound and light people . . . everyone. It mean that I'd shifted most of the cash away from myself come the end of the evening. But the fuckwits didn't know that, so you never knew if some-one was planning to try to take it off you, or just have a go, a revenge attack for something insignificant that happened earlier in the night. We'd be parked around the back of the club for each event and always left together, always in convoy. I'd have a couple of heavy duty guys with crowbars with me, just in case, and I'd only relax when I knew everyone was safe at home. Even then, it was hard to chill, with all the adrenalin still pumping through me.

All I was trying to do was earn a living. That's all. It was a job. Me doing my job meant that other people had jobs and I paid them well; if anything happened to me, jobs were on the line. To

liven the night up and to have a laugh at troublemakers' expense,
I'd tell the lads that they'd get a bonus for the most knock-outs in
a night. It didn't mean that they'd just start hitting punters for the
sake of it, it made them more determined to stop aggro in two
seconds rather than 10 seconds. Seeing a mugger absolutely shit
themselves to be confronted by someone bigger, harder and
scarier than them, always made my night.

Bagleys was a mad venue. Their doormen were all psychos
and we all got on really well with them. They were one of the few
venue security teams who were up for a ruck. Any time there was
any trouble we'd all join forces and break some heads open. It was
so much better having a team of people who were up for it rather
than a few part-timers who were only on the door because they
happened to be big. It was a good venue. You went up this old
cobbled street near Kings Cross and down a hill. There was
nothing else around so once you were there you were there for the
duration. I think that's why there wasn't constant trouble, just a
few people fucking around every now and then. We had a
perimeter fence with doormen who vetted everyone coming in,
then the queue with doormen at intervals, the cash box round the
corner with doormen at each side, and the other corner with metal
detectors and more doormen.

We'd always have around five blokes on the frontline – the
main gate and the cobbled bank out the back was like no man's
land. A firm of at least 20 blokes taunted the boys one night and
ended up getting chased right to the top. As soon as the doormen
walked back to the gate, they were back down after them again,
shouting a good fight, and not having the balls to bring it on. This
time, the gang had got tooled up and they started to walk towards
the doormen looking as menacing as possible. When you've
served in Ireland and killed people for your country, as a few of
my lads had, a 25-year-old hoodie with a club or a broken bottle
is not that scary. No one backed down as they approached. What
the gang didn't know was Mark had just took delivery of some
new American police batons that evening and sold them all to the

security firm. They were extendable polished steel and sounded like a double-barrel shot gun when extended. On the count of three, the batons came out . . . clack, clack . . . 'Chaaaaarge!' I don't think they intended to use them as soon as they did, but a few notches appeared on those batons that night – it was like a scene from *Braveheart*.

We had some geezers outside trying to sell tickets one night. Now, selling tickets outside is not that unusual, but selling stolen ones is. They were stood serving up and selling knock-off tickets down the side street. We knew they were stolen because the shops would pass on the numbers that had been taken, so anyone coming in with them would get stopped. The kids who were bringing them in were obviously not thieves. We still let them in and they told us where they bought them from – Dumb and Dumber stood round the corner.

Me and Gary went to have a word with them. 'Where did you get your tickets from, boys?'

They'd act so fucking hard; I wanted to just smash them up without saying anything. We needed to know we had the right ones though.

'What tickets?' said the taller of the pair.

Gary was a calming influence. 'Come on now,' he said. 'We know you have stolen tickets. Tell us where you got them from, or I'll hit you with my newspaper,' and he brandished his rolled up edition of yesterday's *Guardian* with a grin.

Well, now they were never going to tell us, were they? A fucking rolled up newspaper, you ask? That's right. A rolled up newspaper . . . with concrete in it.

'One last chance,' said Gary.

The guy just grinned, so Gary boshed him on the head. The other one, Dumb, just fucking ran for it as soon as he saw Dumber hit the deck. We took his coat off him and rifled through his pockets for the tickets. While we were there, we took his money and his car keys. Jon Jon came walking round the corner to see if everything was OK. He was too big to run anywhere –

so I chucked him the keys and told him to find out which car belonged to Dumber.

By the time Jon Jon found the car and drove it round the front, the Old Bill were there with us and Alan, the manager of Bagleys, was out too. They told us Dumber's side of the story and we discredited him, saying that he was in possession of stolen tickets, which we could prove, and that he had attacked us when questioned. Any injury he had was through self-defence. They bought it and asked for his coat back. That was when he discovered his car keys were missing . . . exactly when he saw Jon Jon pull up in his car. The Old Bill were torn – now they wanted to know why a 30 stone man was driving the kid's car.

I said, 'We wanted rid of him so we brought the car round to make him leave quicker.'

When Jon Jon squeezed himself out the car, Alan went over to the police to smooth it out properly. He took a photo of the kid and told him it would be kept behind the desk in the cashbox and he'd never be allowed back in.

Gary's *Guardian* became famous. Almost as famous as his manners. That's his nature – a top geezer. He used to patrol the queues outside the rave to keep any trouble down and to chat to people. We saw that he was a good presence to have because he could stop anything that kicked off or persuade anyone not to start, simply by his size. He became an icon – everyone knew him and loved him and his trusty newspaper.

One night, some kids told him they'd just been robbed in the queue and pointed out two geezers who were working their way in and out of the crowds. They sold the kids some tickets, then took them back *and* took the rest of their money. Not a nice thing to do. Gary positioned himself within hearing distance so he could suss out what was going on. The main 'seller' was a Paddy traveller and being aggressive to everyone he spoke to.

'Gentlemen. What are you doing?' asked Gary.

'Fuck off, you black cunt. No one's talking to you,' he said.

If you've seen Guy Ritchie's film *Snatch*, then you'll know

Brad Pitt's character, the traveller with an Irish accent – that's the way this geezer spoke.

'Pardon me?' said Gary.

I was actually stood there at this point, just in case there were a few of them and Gary needed back-up. Not that he needed my help; he would have done four or five guys on his own, no problem. The way this geezer went on was bang out of order. I wanted to jump in but I knew Gary had it all under control. Hearing someone talk to a mate like that makes you want to break their head open. The Gooner was a tough geezer, though, as this bloke would find out in due course.

He turned to Gary, 'No I won't fucking pardon you. You fucking black cunt, you wanker. Go and fuck off like I told you to.'

Some people are brave, and some are just stupid. This idiot squared right up to Gary, losing a good few inches in height, and giving it all his wide-boy traveller-talk. Then he threatened to knock him out unless he fucked off. Inside I was screaming, *Just fucking do him Gary! Make this cunt suffer!*

And Gary was unfazed by it all. What was going on?

The CCTV camera was going on, that's what. Throughout the confrontation, Gary had one eye on the camera as it swept round and was waiting until he was out of frame before making his move. He could see me in his peripheral vision, and he knew what he was going to do. As soon as the camera was at the right point, Gary grabbed his newspaper and cracked the racist, bog-mouthed fucker over the head. He went down like a sack of shit and claret started leaking from his empty skull. I didn't want it to stop there – I was dying to jump in and bash his mate up, but Big Brother was back on the move and Gary was back on patrol like it had never happened. I think he just fell over, officer.

People just stepped over him and his claret. I leaned over and looked at the sparko gypsy. 'I bet you won't call him a black cunt again,' I said.

Everyone within earshot cracked up laughing. The police arrived and it turned out that of all the hundreds of people in that queue, no one saw anything happen.

We had a lot of ticket problems everywhere. We used people on the fringes of our group of mates to keep eyes out for us. We'd put up with them selling tickets as long as they'd tell us if they bought any stolen ones. Books of tickets went missing from shops all the time so they'd be doing us a favour. We would tell them which numbers to look out for and sure enough, the time came when one of them bought some knock-off tickets and used one of the firm's radios to tell the lads on the door what the sellers looked like. It was a good set up. The amount of stolen tickets we recovered and people we smashed up as a result of our snitch was amazing.

There was a funny one at Bagleys. I was sat in the cash box with my mum, she was doing her thing and I was writing all the wages books out for the night. It always used to give me the hump.

A punter came up to the counter and started arguing and haggling over the price and my mum said, 'This is how much it costs. Pay it or leave.'

I wasn't really paying too much attention until she raised her voice. Then the geezer spoke back and called her a cunt. I looked up from my paperwork for a second and thought, *Nah, he didn't just say that. I imagined it.*

Back to work, and I heard him say it again. Mum turned to see my empty chair. When she spun back to look at the geezer I had him pinned to the wall by his throat and was punching him in the face with my right. It was a red mist moment and I didn't want to stop. His nose was burst open and after three follow-up big rights to his face, I let him fall to the floor and then cracked him again. When you're in that frame of mind, no one can stop you – I was like a fucking animal. The doormen came over and when I told them what he'd said, they laid into him as well. My mum wasn't happy with us. 'Terry,' she said. 'I was quite capable of dealing with him myself. Everything was under control. Give me my coat, I'm going home!'

Things like that – funny as they were – helped to solidify the doubts in my head. How much longer did I want to be doing this? When would my – our – luck run out? I started running clubs to make money out of something that I loved and, at times, particularly in the early days, it was the best job in the world. The downside to all the great people I was meeting was that I encountered some really nasty bastards and the sort of evil people you think just exist in films.

The whole scene was changing. Once, it had been stand-up people and kids out for a good time. But the money was always going to pull in scum. It was full of idiots, chancers and con men, muggers and drug dealers . . . and those were the nice ones. There were too many negative elements. No one other than my own team was interested in getting along or doing a favour unless there was a motive behind it.

I'd get offered drugs at every club I went to, mainly by punters. It got to the stage where it was all people would do – see me, say hello, and offer me some pills or coke, trying to befriend me. It was embarrassing. I always said no – apart from anything, I couldn't afford the hassle it might bring. If I took a pill off someone, just to get rid of them, and got searched that night I'd get banged up. A fellow promoter or the venue owner buying me a bottle of champagne, that was fine – that's what went on and it was accepted. Accepting something from a punter would only mean they'd ask for a favour in return.

In my earlier days, there was this geezer who offered me some gear. I declined his offer and let him buy me a drink instead. I said I'd have whatever he was having and we shared a bottle of shampoo and had a right laugh. Not too long after, there were police on the doors of a club checking every third or fourth person coming in. It was a routine thing that they did every blue moon and my champagne-buying friend was dragged out the queue to be searched. He shouted for me, asking me what was going on. I told him not to go shouting my name around like that. The police were actually doing us a good turn, so I didn't want some idiot like him messing it up. After searching him, they found a load of gear and it was obvious that he was a dealer. I had no idea and was not happy that he'd tried to befriend me under false pretences. The police told me he kept name-dropping me and said that I'd sort everything out for him. In his tiny world, maybe. Not in mine. I told them the score and that I didn't even know his fucking name. That was the flipside of being Mr Popular.

Another one was all these mugs who'd go throwing my name about when they got themselves into trouble. It was the *I'll speak to Terry about you* shit that put me in a few awkward positions.

I used to get calls from people saying, 'Mr Muppet says you'll do this to us if we sort him out. Is it true?'

Of course it wasn't true. I'd tell them I knew nothing about it, didn't care about it, and they were quite free to give the geezer a smack in the mouth without any interference from me. In fact, I'd usually tell them to get an extra one in from me while they were at it. I'd always phone the name-dropper and tell them their plan had backfired and they were going to get a clump.

Everyone with a reputation for fighting or violence or not taking any shit from people has been plagued with this one. I could say hello to someone in a club and they'd think they were connected to me. It was dangerous. I've never been interested in getting myself mixed up in that kind of rubbish. The perfect example is a 'mate' owed some geezers some money and refused to pay them.

They got the hump and said, 'Pay up or you're fucked,' and he said that I'd smash them up if they laid a finger on him.

So by knowing me, he thought he could get out of owing someone money, and bring me in as his heavy mob. When the geezers phoned me to confirm my intentions, I told them they could do whatever they wanted and had my blessing to do it. I'd never beat someone up as a favour to anyone. If they are so desperate, they can pay someone to do it. I think it's offensive for a so-called mate to do something like that to you. A real mate of mine just wouldn't have done it.

Maybe I sound like an old fogey, going on about how much better it was in the old days. But those old days are not that far away – the thing that gets to me is how the violence progressed and fucked it all up. And it's getting worse. There's been loads of shootings in clubs.

First it was idiots settling scores. Then it was guys on the door. I could see that, before long, promoters were going to be targeted. Sadly, I was right: just as we were finishing this book, Peter Oduwole, the guy behind Cosa Nostra, was blown away while he was out flyering.

That could have been me.

A NEW CHAPTER

With most things in life, somewhere along the line you stop enjoying it as much as you used to. I'd had the wildest and best experiences of my life when I was connected to the scene, doing more in those years that some people do in a lifetime. But it couldn't last forever.

How many mad-for-it ravers do you see in their 30s? Very few – most of them have settled down to their jobs and families. The ones who haven't – I salute you, but I think you're fucking nuts.

Promoting's much the same. Yes, you get women throwing themselves at you. Yes, it's great when your job is to be out all night partying, listening to your favourite music. Yes, the money's good.

The problem for me was this.

First, I'd settled down with Max – she had our son, Alfie, recently – so I had no interest in the other birds any more.

Second, I'd gone off the music. I knew I'd changed when I'd find myself thinking, What the *fuck* is this *shit*?' It really got right on my tits. I wasn't a pilled-up 20-year-old and couldn't identify with it all anymore. A magazine interviewed me towards the end, and asked me about my favourite music. I started telling them I liked Frank Sinatra and Luther Vandross. The writer interrupted me. 'No, your favourite *rave* music.'

'Rave music?' I said. And I though for a minute. 'D'you know,' I said. 'I fucking hate it, now. I think it's shit.'

The tape packs, a good source of income, had become painful

for me. I had to listen to each one, all the way through, before it went out to make sure it was recorded properly and sounded the bollocks. Early on, I'd loved that – I'd have them on in the car, driving to and from record shops . . . it wasn't a chore. Now, I was finding it murder to listen to it all. It was taking me a week to get through one set of tapes – literally, it was a load of noise, banging sounds with some geezer shouting rubbish over the top of it – and turning me into a grumpy old man, for fuck's sake.

Worst of all, I didn't even know if it was even any good – I mean, in terms of whether the kids would like it – any more. And you can't promote something if you're not into it – it soon shows.

And what about the money? Well, that wasn't as good as it had been, either. At the peak, I'd been earning 250 to 300 grand a year. Not bad for a lad from the Old Dean, who'd never made it higher than lobby host of a McDonalds working for anyone else. But the peak was gone and I was looking at a major downturn. I've already mentioned Ibiza and Ayia Napa, where any old tit was turning up and running nights in clubs for a drink and a shag. Most of the nights were shit, but the punters were pilled up or pissed and didn't really care. I've also mentioned the fucking DJs. At first, DJs were grateful for the break I was giving them. They'd all have shitty day jobs and could be a hero for an hour at one of our raves. These bedroom DJs had no track record, no following, and no bargaining tools but that started to change as more and more events happened. Because most of them were arrogant little shits to begin with, the tiniest amount of recognition just took their egos higher and higher. They quickly got caught up in the scene and all the hype that went with it and thought they were something they weren't. They started demanding more money and were more and more unreliable each week. As the scene grew, there were more promoters putting on more events on all the time. DJs and MCs could pick and choose where they wanted to play and 'play' is what they did. They played promoters off against each other, agreeing to one gig and then double-booking themselves to hold out for the most money and let people down –

there was no honour and being dropped in the shit was something we all came to expect. A lot of them began turning up 20 minutes late and wanting to leave 20 minutes early and would start throwing their toys out their pram when I said I'd take a hundred quid from their fee.

It wasn't just them. Everyone wanted more dough – the venue owners wanted to double their fees, the sound system people wanted to treble theirs, the printers kept moaning about paper costs, the lighting costs went up, the laser companies charged the earth, even the doormen wanted in on it. As a promoter, I couldn't charge any more money for tickets than I was. No one would pay it. So I was getting squeezed, big-time.

It had never been about the money for me – I liked having it and I liked spending it, but I was at my happiest when I had the real passion for raving – but I couldn't do it for nothing. It all combined to kill the passion and when that goes, you've got to call it a day.

In the beginning, I was giving clubbers what I knew they wanted from my own experience. It worked – I was spot on. The raves had my personal stamp, I was so in touch with the culture and that's why they became so popular. My thinking was that it was easy – I couldn't see how other promoters didn't know what their punters would like. You have to know your audience or you're fucked. Now, I was drifting away from my audience.

The thing which eventually made up my mind was the violence, the guns and crackheads. I said earlier, I never enjoyed the fighting – even though sometimes it might sound like I did. I got a sort of satisfaction out of kicking the shit out of muggers but it was only a means to an end – the end being the safety and well-being of my punters and our events. Given the choice, I'd have rather stayed at home with a glass of claret than spill the stuff all over a dancefloor in Dalston. When I was a young kid raving, the worst you'd get was a hug off a bloke and a shag off a woman. No one sold moody drugs, and shooting and stabbing was unheard of. By the time I started promoting, muggers with knives were everywhere. Around 2000, things got even worse. Every other fucker was doing lines of coke – before, it had been mainly ecstasy, amphetamines and puff, none of which is likely to send you too yampy – and the smell of crack being smoked was always hanging around in the air. Crack, particularly, is a funny fucking drug: it makes people hyper-aggressive, totally paranoid and completely unreasonable. That's a nasty combination when the cunt in question's got a 9mm stuffed down the back of his ridiculously low-slung pants. I'm not frightened of anyone, but I have no desire to be fucking shot dead by a 17-year-old toe rag because he's off his face, he wants to get into my club for free and I've said no.

I've talked about the times we kicked the fuck out of people for threatening us with guns. I actually had them pulled on me three times, and the time it happened at the Rex in Stratford was probably the maddest. About a month prior to this, someone shot the place up for being refused entry and one of the doormen ended up in intensive care. He was wearing a bullet-proof vest at the time and ended up with a bullet in his collar bone. Another bullet hit the bird in the cash box in the arm – a bird, for fuck's sake. Any other time that could have been my mum in there, which was a wake-up call in itself. Anyway, three big, tough, black geezers wanted to get in to the Rex and they refused to be searched. OK, if that's what you want, then you're not coming in. I'd refuse to let my best mates in without being searched, so a few scumbags weren't going to just stroll in and bring in whatever they wanted. The rules were quite simple. We were on edge because of the shooting – especially wary of any threats from people being knocked back.

They were arguing with one of the lads on the door and wouldn't let it go. Other punters were getting agitated by it, the real punters who wanted to get inside to listen to music and to dance, the kind who had no interest in hardman gangster talk. I was just inside the foyer, not too far from the door and could see and hear it all happening.

'Do you know who we is innit?' asked one.

'We gon be back to see yas, boy,' said another. It was getting me riled because they should have just been turned away without discussion, and also because of the atmosphere it was creating. The longer the doorman was conversing with them, the more time they had to suss out who was where if they were going to shoot it up.

Also, people couldn't just walk round them to get in, it was holding the line up and everyone could hear the threats that the three geezers started coming out with – not just towards the doormen, but to everyone in the building.

I shouted over, 'Just tell them to *fuck off*,' and followed it up by telling them myself.

If they didn't move away from the door immediately, they'd get hurt. It shut them up and they wanted a staring contest in return ... '*Fuck off you cunts!*' helped them on their way, shuffling off with their tails between their legs.

One of the geezers turned and said, 'You don know who we is.'

If I never heard, 'Do you know who I am?' ever again, it would be too soon.

My standard answer was always going to be, 'I don't give a fuck who you are.'

I didn't need to know these three geezers to know they were a set of wankers. I stood in their way, looking each of them in the eye and told them to move it for the last time. Of course, that wasn't the end of it.

Stood across the road, with the safety of 30 yards of Tarmac between us, they started shouting the odds. 'You gon die,' said one.

Brilliant. Death threats, when we're stood next to a fuck-off luminous yellow sign about a shooting the previous week. It was very uncomfortable for the punters and I could see them having second thoughts about being stuck in east London in the middle of a shoot-out. One thing I found disturbing was the inability of these fuckwits to talk properly. They were from Peckham or somewhere – born and bred in London. So what's with all the Ali G, Jamaica-crossed-with-Compton bollocks? We were used to them talking like that; we used an interpreter for the first few months until we learned idiot-speak.

Anyway, we couldn't just leave that threat hanging in the air.

I grabbed a couple of doormen and went over to confront them.

'Look guys,' I said, 'I'll say it again so you can understand. You can come in, but only after we've searched you. No one gets in otherwise.'

They replied with, 'You don know who we . . .'

I cut him down. 'Look. I couldn't give a *fuck* who you are, you silly cunt,' I said, losing my temper, wanting to take his face off there and then.

'Come here and say that,' one of them replied.

Try fucking stopping me. I had an extendable cosh in my pocket and I was ready to knock this fucker's teeth out.

I had it in my hand, in my pocket, poised. 'Come on then, you cunt.' I said. 'Let's fucking have it.'

He started backing into an alley, with me following. In my mind, I just needed him to walk far enough down there and I'd kick the shit out of him in seconds. Of course, he had a different scenario in his mind. As we walked he took his gun out and held it by his side.

I thought it was a knife and it just made me angrier, goading him, 'What the fuck you gonna do with that then, eh?'

I flicked my cosh out, ready to mess him up. With both weapons on show, I knew I could take him if he lunged at me.

My mate Mark had realised what was going on. 'He's got a gun, Tel,' he said. '*He's got a gun.*'

It didn't sink in at first, but then I saw the glint of what little street light there was on the barrel and realised what Mark was saying. A fucking gun. *Shit.* I'd just walked down an alley with some scumbag who's carrying a gun. Ambushed. My tactics switched and I started backing off, trying to bring him out of the alley.

'What you gonna shoot me for, then?' I said. 'For not letting you in a club?'

Trying to make it sound such a small thing – which it was – might just make him decide against using it.

'Come on. You don't want to want to shoot me, do you? That's too fucking serious. We can all just walk away from this.'

All the time, he was saying, 'Don't make me use it.'

Which gave me some hope he didn't really want to. A few seconds later, I'd edged back onto the street, he'd followed and his face was caught on the CCTV camera. He fucked off and was nicked later.

I'd come fucking close. If I'd gone to hit the cunt, or Mark hadn't spotted the gun, I might have caught one between the eyes. It was frightening, genuinely.

With the way the scene was going, there were two things I could see happening: someone *would* shoot me, or someone would get killed for threatening to shoot me. Either way, it wasn't a great prognosis. My life was in danger or I'd go to prison for a long time.

Even if I'd not thought that, Maxine would have made my mind up for me. She came to a few events to sample what I did for a living – Garage Nation at the Sanctuary and a weekender at Butlins in Kent. Talk about a culture shock. It was probably the first time in history that anyone had walked through Butlins with a Louis Vuitton suitcase. She hated the music and she hated the idiots who were out to spoil everything. She'd heard a lot of stories from me, but she'd grown up sheltered, in a bubble, and she didn't really understand what these cunts were actually like. Seeing it, first-hand, with her own eyes, shocked her. It worried her, too, and having her there – worrying about her, unable to relax in case someone mugged her or attacked her – made me look at it in a new light. She was pregnant, too. 'I'm having your baby, this has got to stop,' she said.

It wasn't her spoiling my fun and giving me an ultimatum. She was telling me what I already knew, giving me good advice, something that I'd not had too much of in my life. She hated seeing me running around in that shit. The decision was a lot easier because I was moving away from the scene and towards a different, grown-up way of life.

Towards the end of 2002, I put the word around that I was open to offers for One Nation and Garage Nation, speaking to a few people who were on our level.

I got a lot of interest.

One was from this prick who thought he'd lay down the law to me. 'I'm making you this offer,' he said, naming a figure. 'But this is the only offer I'm making. I'm not getting into an auction. If you get a better offer don't come back asking me to go higher.'

I did get a better offer, from Mike and Grant, who run Slammin Vinyl and had also bought United Dance off Chris Brown. The deal was concluded very quickly. I got a nice fat cheque and they got the UK's best club promotion business (in my opinion).

The prick phoned me back a week or two later. 'You've fucking sold it,' he said. 'Why didn't you come back to see if I'd offer you more than them?'

What a cunt. I must arrange a game of high stakes poker with him one of these days.

My last event was in February 2003. Funnily enough, it was the one where MC Navigator and his two mates navigated themselves the fuck out of the Brixton Academy after the row about his fees. I was glad to be leaving all these pricks behind but it was an emotional night, a really good, buzzing party, with 5,000 people there and a camera crew recording it all for posterity. I gave up something I love, walking out on a 15 year relationship, which was not an easy thing to do. It was a huge risk to leave that all behind to pursue something else, but it was a decision I made and stood by. I was called up on stage to say my goodbyes; I stood there, looking out over thousands of Cheesy Quavers, and wondered if I'd done the right thing. Was I brave, or a fool? I'd never know unless I made the move. I got an amazing send-off – the south London lads wanted to give a gun salute at the end, but we couldn't let them do it. How the fuck did they get guns in anyway?

Afterwards, I was driving home at six in the morning; the sun was coming up, the day just beginning and I was on my way back to bed.

I actually smiled to myself and thought, *I don't have to go to another rave ever again*. I don't have to worry about muggers and gunmen in my parties again. I don't have to listen to shit music at 150db again. I don't have to listen to people telling me they're the next big thing and shouting some rubbish in my ear, or smile politely as I take demo tapes of crap from useless DJs, or deal with all the egos and attitudes. I don't have to wear a bullet proof vest to work. I don't have to worry about aggravation from the Tax Man and the VAT people.

I'd got out just in time, before the frustration and dislike of the scene I'd once loved turned to hatred.

Everything was lifted from my shoulders. For the first time in a decade, I could relax.

We went out for dinner that night and I reclaimed my life.

Of course, me being me, there's loads I miss about the scene, too. Terry Turbo *was* One Nation. I put my heart and soul into each and every event and I lost something special when I sold it all on. Mainly, I miss the satisfaction you get when you're there at midnight, everyone's in, the party's in full swing, there's no trouble and everyone's having a good time. You stand on stage, you look out at the crowd, and you think, fuck me, I created this.

I miss a lot of the people. I miss the clubbers, most of them were great – and if you're reading this, thanks for everything. I miss a few of the DJs and MCs, and a few of the venue owners. Of course, I miss the Team – we're still in touch, most of us, and they're all doing different things now . . . running their own businesses, doing doors elsewhere, chilling. But none of them have worked anywhere like it since and I'm glad I was able to create that kind of unity. The scrapes we'd been in gave us a unique bond – we'd have done anything for each other. I know they'd have taken a bullet for me and I'd have done the same for them. I miss the banter and the crack (the laughs, not the stuff you smoke) we had together.

I miss the money, but I made loads more money outside clubs than in them. Most of the serious dough I made was in property: from that first little council flat, I ended up with 13 houses at one point, surfing the boom all the way up.

Me and the boys have been talking lately: we need to get together and go out clubbing together again. I've got that itch. Don't know when or where, but watch out for us – we'll be the gang of silly geezers having a laugh and making tits of ourselves. Possibly with earplugs in.

One Nation and Garage Nation taught me a lot of things, most of which sound like clichés but they're true.

First, a winner never quits, and a quitter never wins.

Second, we learn from our mistakes. God knows I made enough of them, in and out of the clubs. I got greedy sometimes, listened to my wallet not my head.

Third, there's no such thing as a get rich quick scheme. If you want something in life, you have to graft for it. I lost a lot of money in the Stock Market making that mistake. I used to put 6k away in a PEP – I bet I was the only rave promoter who did, as well – and, after four years, the guy said to me, 'It's worth 36k now.' Well, that's a nice earner. Tax-free, too. That got me interested. A mate of mine suggested an investment in Europe. I put 20k in, and six months later it was worth 40k. I thought, Fuck me, this is easy. So I piled in. I was sticking money into tech stocks, the Pacific Rim, high risk this, low risk that. I banged another 80 grand in and just forgot about it. That's great, that's safe, it's going to double in the next year, game on. I thought I'd made it.

Then we came to the Millennium night disaster and I needed to pull my money out to help fund my recovery. And fuck me, it had all dropped. The 10ks and 20ks had vanished, the 80 was now worth 40. I took a right cold bath.

I've done a fortune on cars, too, but that's different. I used to change my car each year, and waved goodbye to between 5k and 15k each time on depreciation. But I love cars and I love new ones best of all. They were my main vice, really.

A lot of people ask me what I'd have done if I hadn't gone into promoting. The truth is, I'm not sure. Probably something to do with sales: I'm a people person, I could have done OK in that. The older you get, the more you realise what the real priorities in life are. I still like living in a nice house and driving a nice car, and I like nice clothes. But the fact is, I reckon I'd have been just as happy settled down with Max in my 20s, with a couple of kids, a semi-detached and a company Mondeo. Family's what makes you happy, stability and people around you that you love. You can't buy that in any shop in the world.

Of course, a lot of my mates from school drifted into crime. I know enough naughty people to have been able to find myself a job of some description in that line, but that wasn't for me. Don't do the crime if you can't do the time – that was a motto I always understood. People used to say, 'You must be knocking out the gear, Terry . . . all those ravers and you're not supplying them their Es?'

Yeah . . . and go to prison for 15 years? What do you think I am? A muppet? I've seen and known too many criminals and I know it's a mug's game.

So much for what I *would* have done. What about what I am doing?

Well, I'm acting now. I got the bug when I appeared on *Britain's Angriest Men*. There was me and other two geezers, both of whom needed help more than anything: basically, they just went around talking themselves into a battering. One of them sat there surrounded by Argos garden furniture talking about fighting and beating people up when he had road rage. In his own world, he was Conan the Barbarian . . . in the real world, he was

Norman the Sagittarian, who wouldn't last five minutes in a row with anyone other than his reflection. In the programme, I took the cameras around with me to acting and singing classes, and to the raves. Of course, at the raves I *was* angry and they just picked all the bits out they wanted to, so I was angry all the time. As a result, I had no auditions for a year. People weren't interested in case I lost my rag on set. It was another learning experience.

I changed my agent, and my name – I act as Terry Stone, now, because Terry Turbo sounds a bit like a Panto villain. Eventually, auditions did come in. Thank fuck. I've been on *The Bill*, *My Family* and was lucky enough to have been the geezer who beat Alfie Moon up in *Eastenders*. I've also had starring roles in three feature films: *One Man And His Dog*, with the darts legend and all-round great guy Bobby George, *Hell to Pay* with Dave Courtney and Billy Murray, and the award-winning *Rollin' with the Nines*, in next to no time at all.

Acting's the hardest game I've ever been in in my life. With most things, you work, you advertise, something happens. With acting, it takes a lot longer. People think Orlando Bloom came out of drama school and went straight to LA. Bollocks. He's been acting since 1992 – he's done Bloke no2 who walks on and walks off in *Casualty* and that's the way you have to work. So I'm in it for the long-haul. And, as ever, I'm optimistic. I got great reviews for my performance in *Rollin' With The Nines* and I've already done more in four years than loads of people who've been acting for 20.

It's different from raving, but I'm different from the geezer I was 15 years ago, so that's only right.

I hope you too got as much as I did from an amazing scene and you've enjoyed this little trip down memory lane. I also hope that it's been an insight into what I put myself through and how determination will always get you where you want to be.

If there's a message to be left with, I want it to be this – make the most of what you've got. There is a lot more to fighting than just beating someone up – a fighter is someone who never gives up in life and keeps on pushing through the good times and the bad and following their heart and mind into the unknown. Finding what you want in life, happiness, a bird, a job, nice car, house, inner peace, can be done.

If you believe in yourself, you can do it. You can make it happen if you want it bad enough. I'm living proof.

CAST OF CHARACTERS

Wilf Pine – The One and Only.
Richard Williams.
Marvellous Marvin Cain.
Nigel Green.
Russell and Danny, The Flying Squad.
Kenny and Noah, Living Dream.
Danielle and Rochelle, DJs and *Scene* writers.
Chris Brown, United Dance.
Andy, Mark, Phil and Mick, partners in my early days.
John and Andrew Searchfield, owners of The Rhythm Station at Aldershot and all-round good guys.
Jason Kaye, DJ, legend and Garage Nation partner.
Mikey B, Radio One's Dreem Team (and part of Top Buzz with Jase).
Fabio and Grooverider – DJs and mates from my days at The Rhythm Station.
Slipmatt. Top geezer.
Goldie.
Bradley Carter.
Bolino.
Dougal.
Vinyl Groover.
DJ Sy.
Ellis D.
Joe Deacon.
George Bowie.
QWX.
Bass Instinct.
Mikey B.

King of Clubs

Tizer.
Brisk.
MC MC.
DJ Trix.
Christian.
MC Cyanide.
Frances Williams, account and Godsend.
Daniella Westbrook, Ali G, David Beckham and The Queen – One Nation punters (sort of).
The Late Murray Beetson, Dreamscape. Good friend. RIP.
The Team and associates: Warrior, Gary Gooner, Adam Saint, Boogie, Billie, Jon Jon, Mr Magoo (RIP), Jeremy Bailey, Matt and The Animal, Mark aka RS, Nick and Bruscoe, Scooby, Big Albert, Ken and Jim, Eddie Stokes, Terry Fisher, Pikki and Temper, Pinto and Tuffy, Felix. Apologies if I've missed anyone out – you were all total legends.
Carlton Leach, Essex Connection and good mate.
Illayas, the Mallas's, George, John Davis – business associates from Ibiza and Ayia Napa.
Puff Daddy – drinking buddy. Seriously.
Mega Man and Romeo, good mates from the So Solid Crew.
Dave Courtney, gangster, author, mate.
Roy Shaw, Freddie Foreman, Tony Lambrianou, Bruce Reynolds, Charlie Richardson, the Nashes, Frank Fraser and Joey Pyle – some of the top people I was lucky enough to meet through Dave.
Iks. Don't ask.
Um Foo Foo. Also don't ask.
Fishy Lips. Ditto.
Bernado Provenzano. Another name for Terry Turbo, according to some.
Maxine. Perhaps the only sane woman in the world. She's beautiful, too.
Alfie and Jade. My baby boy and my little girl.
Anne Walker and Vicky Yorke.
Mike and Grant from Slammin Vinyl. Top boys.
Bill Murray, actor and business partner.
Bobby George, actor and darts legend.
Terry Stone. Me.